BIBLIOHOLISM

THE LITERARY ADDICTION

BIBLIOHOLISM

THE LITERARY ADDICTION

REVISED EDITION

Tom Raabe

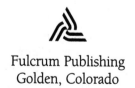

Fulcrum Publishing
Golden, Colorado

To Mom and Dad

Library of Congress Cataloging-in-Publication Data

Raabe, Tom.
   Biblioholism : the literary addiction / Tom Raabe.—Rev. ed.
        p. cm.
Includes bibliographical references.
   ISBN 1-55591-240-0
   1. Bibliomania. 2. Bibliography. 3. Book collecting. 4. Books and
reading. 5. Bibliomania—Humor. 6. Bibliography—Humor. 7. Book
collecting—Humor. 8. Books and reading—Humor. I. Title.
   Z992 .R25 2001
   002'.074—dc21   2001000198

Printed in the United States of America
      0 9 8 7 6 5 4 3 2 1

Project editor: Daniel Forrest-Bank
Editorial: Marlene Blessing, Erin Lawson
Design: cb graphics, Constance Bollen
Cover illustration: Arthur Asa Berger

Fulcrum Publishing
16100 Table Mountain Parkway, Suite 300
Golden, Colorado 80403
(800) 992-2908 • (303) 277-1623
www.fulcrum-books.com

Contents

Contents

Acknowledgments

THE EFFORTS OF MANY BIBLIOHOLICS—some of them in advanced stages of denial—went into the making of this book. And, while it is probably best not to encourage them, in the long run the only help low-bottom bookaholics like these folks are going to get must come from within. Getting in their faces about their condition isn't going to help one iota. So, at the risk of offending the local Book-Anon chapter, I acknowledge them.

These unfortunate individuals are Bob Baron, who must reap partial credit for allowing the lineaments of this hideous disease to see the black of ink. It was his idea to expand to a book-length essay material I had considered only fertile enough for a newspaper article. He also supplied a number of jokes (the ones you laugh at are probably his). Add to that the efforts of the Fulcrum staff, especially Cara Smedley, Linda Stark, Carmel Huestis, Karen Groves, Daniel Forrest-Bank and Jay Staten (who has the disease *real* bad; anybody whose first inclination while seated in an airborne jetliner that has just developed engine trouble is to read Thomas Mann's *Magic Mountain* is beyond help). Finally, admit the insightful comments (and friendly prodding) of Marlene Blessing, and the biblioholic musings of Johanna Bierwirth and of the brave people who bared their biblioholic souls by returning a rather hurriedly conceived survey, and the truth about this hideous condition can finally be told.

Preface

WHEN TOM RAABE'S HUMOROUS LOOK at the passion—no make that *obsession*—for finding, reading, and collecting books was first published a decade ago, the landscape of book publishing and bookselling was in flux, but still a recognizable place. The neighborhood independent bookstore remained a viable enterprise, a regular hangout for bibliophiles, those who craved the dustier volumes in darkest and most wonderful corners of the store.

We need waste no space, Dear Reader, in telling you about the influence that today's megastores wield in the marketplace of books. Of course, it is not just the simulated comfort of a newly remodeled living room in each of these stores that characterizes them. To be profitable, such stores require a steady stream of best-selling books to retail, something that has profoundly influenced what gets published (and conversely, what doesn't). In return, this has provided publishers with sales volume that, at least on the surface, seems a boon to the bottom line of a risky business.

Just as we start to quake a little about the dimmed prospect of finding Cervantes' *Don Quixote* on our bookstore shelves (or maybe something slightly more obscure, such as Flaubert's *A Sentimental Education* or Emily Bronte's *Villette*), we hear a distant trumpet that promises a revolution of a powerful order. The highest note sounded is the E-note: E-publishing, E-books, E-tailing a la Amazon.com, E-libraries from which subscribers and subscriber institutions (libraries, schools and businesses) can download a large inventory of titles. Holy guacamole! This sounds strange, but perhaps promising.

To bring his unique perspective (and more than a few suspicions) to some of the possibilities that await us—or that will be taking place as we peacefully sleep in our beds—Tom Raabe has added a final chapter, an Afterword (but surely not the last word) to *Biblioholism: The Literary Addiction*. In it, he explores some of the questions that the electronic age brings to the making—and acquisition—of books.

As always, Tom has his predilections. He has not loosened his grip on the real book, as opposed to the virtual book. He likes paper and inked typography, all bound together by stitching or glue and surrounded by an artful cover, soft or hard. As do most of you who will read and relish this book. Even the publishing pundits, who have a cautiously optimistic view of what it will mean to be able to keep books in print indefinitely and to offer readers all books all the time, have their belief that traditional books (called by some P-books for their paper platform) will always exist. "Books as physical objects will not pass away to be replaced by electronic signals read from glowing, hand-held screens. Nor will bookstores vanish," posits Jason Epstein in his freshly minted title, *Book Business: Publishing Past Present and Future*. The same sentiment is uttered by cyber-critic Sven Birkerts, with just a touch of impending shadow: "Books will exist, of course, and they will have their special uses, but they will be like those older roads we find everywhere running parallel to the big interstates."

Why the preoccupation with the business of books, once and future, and the worry about printed books becoming mere back roads? Because, Book Lovers, it has everything to do with where you'll find your books and in what forms, something that has remained relatively constant from the time of Gutenberg and his movable type printing press until now. Revel with Tom as you delight in the pages ahead. You are sure to find your own biblioholic profile. And then, perhaps, retreat

Preface

to a comforting corner in which to imbibe his look at the future of books in his Epilogue. You may discover that you embrace a dual world, in which some books are real, while others are virtual, mere bits or bytes of digitized information. Or you may, like your Fearless Leader Tom Raabe, simply click your heels together a few times and say "There's no place like books."

—Marlene Blessing
Editor-in-Chief, Fulcrum Publishing
January 2001

CHAPTER ONE

Confessions of a Biblioholic

What wild desires, what restless torments seize
The hapless man, who feels the book-disease.[1]

DO YOU HAVE A BOOKSTORE PROBLEM? Have you ever strolled breezily into a bookstore with the singular intention of killing a few minutes of time, only to exit many hours later with more than a few volumes tucked under your arm? Does simply being amid thousands upon thousands of neatly stacked and attractively displayed books leave you mysteriously exhilarated? Does it make you feel good? Maybe too good?

If the answer to these questions is yes, you may have some hard and difficult times ahead of you. I know. I have been there. I have sampled the esoteric delights. I know of their seductive and unrelinquishing power.

I am a biblioholic.

Don't laugh. It is a malady more common than one might expect, capable of bringing even the most circumspect into its grasp. After all, who has not experienced a certain ebullience of spirit upon entering a sizable bookstore, a feeling of being snatched up from the freneticism of workaday life and deposited into a quieter, saner world, a sanctuary where intellect and grand ideas are allowed free rein? Who has not fed that euphoria with grandiose purchases? Who has not longed to return? As I said, I know. It happened to me. And it can happen to you, too.

My travail began as all such travails begin—with browsing. Blowing into a store, roaming the stacks, and blowing out again, toting perhaps a tome or two of standard and popular fare: the most recent *Far Side Gallery*, maybe, or the latest from Tom Clancy. Fun, certainly; interesting, indeed; and for the most part, perfectly normal human behavior. Everybody goes to the bookstore once in a while. Everybody drops a few bucks on something to read in the spare moments.

Little did I recognize the subtle mood change that accompanied my visits, the stimulation of my intellectual curiosity, the association of the stacks with inner peace, the rhapsodic joy of pulling out a shiny paperback and carrying it through the door. I was quite innocently getting high, laying the foundation for an addictive relationship that was to bedevil my every waking hour.

Sunday afternoons were my favorite time in those early days. At first sporadically, but with increasing regularity, I spent those hours capering euphorically about the corridors of knowledge and wisdom at my favorite bookstore. I wasn't buying extravagantly in those early days. My needs were met by the mere proximity of the volumes. I strolled the aisles and read the titles; I pulled volumes off the shelves and flipped through the pages; I admired the cover art and took in the contours of the tomes. I wanted to know it all; I wanted to read them all. There is something about the proximity of all that knowledge, the nearness of all that great writing, the smell of all those books, that is intoxicating in the extreme. I wanted to be near them. I wanted everything about them to osmose directly into my brain.

And soon I wanted to buy them. My first serious buying sprees occurred in the Tattered Cover Book Store, the Chivas Regal of Denver-area stores. When I first walked among its cornucopic selection, its nook-and-cranny interior, its nimiety of overstuffed chairs, I walked as one enveloped in karmic bliss. I knew I would be a "regular" before my body was halfway through the door. It was commonplace for me to "veg out" in its corners, consuming half a novel here, a sociological treatise there. And half a day later I'd emerge strangely enlivened, with fifty dollars' worth of books under my arm, giddily oblivious to the world and all its problems.

This weekly hegira continued through the spring and summer of that year, and although I perceived my behavior as encroaching upon addiction, I allowed it to run unabated, thinking it would die a happy death come September and the intervening counterintoxicant of professional football.

By summer's end, however, I was hooked big time. I missed the entire 1998 season. But—and this is the debilitating danger of the condition—Sunday afternoons could no longer satiate my hunger. I came back on weekday evenings, and as time went by I began to increase my purchases. Moreover, my taste in bookstores became far more eclectic. Waldenbooks, Barnes & Noble, Borders, various leading used bookstores—it didn't matter. I was there. And I was spending money.

Certainly, many of my purchases were from the bargain shelf, where my raging conscience could be muted by the rationalization that a $14.95 tome reduced to $2.95 was a necessity regardless of the subject of the volume. Many, many volumes can be purchased under such pretenses. Books you know you will never read. Books that, for some ineffable reason, momentarily pricked your soul and before you knew it you were at home pulling them out of your sack and wondering *how . . . why.*

I have amassed, for example, a personal library of untold volumes of poetry—unperused, untouched—and I no better understand poetry than I do the NBA illegal-defense rule. Burton Raffel's *How to Read a Poem* sits awaiting future consumption on my shelves—in triplicate.

However, for the biblioholic, bargain books are never enough. The craving extends to full-priced tomes as well, few of which, unfortunately, can be found on the dollar-a-pound table. And, for the biblioholic, any reason can be found to buy them. He or she may buy a volume simply to learn more about a given subject. It's not necessary to read it immediately. Just having it on the shelf, the biblioholic is deluded into thinking, may help one grow intellectually.

That's one of the insidious things about this disease. Buying becomes a sort of vicarious learning experience. One would dearly love to absorb the knowledge that lies buried between the covers of all the books that pique one's interest in a bookstore. But of course, that would involve sitting oneself down, laboring through the tome, chalking up hour upon hour of heavy intellectual toil. And, well, who has time for that? I mean, people have to work and piddle around the house on weekends and some have kids to take care of and everything else.

For example, I'd love to learn of the provenance of James Joyce's particular afflatus. I'd dearly love to bury myself in the abstruse mythological allusions and the cryptic Irish associations of his later fiction. In short, I'd love to devote two or three years of my life to figuring out what the heck the guy was trying to say. But, realistically, I don't have time to do it. I have a life to live too. So I buy his books and books about him. I admire the covers. I flip through the pages, checking the indexes here, scanning a paragraph there, and I lay plans to read them from start to end. But then I never do. Other subjects, other books, entice my attention, and I must move on, purchasing different tomes, admiring different covers, flipping through different pages.

However, book buying did not include a continual euphoria in those early days. There was guilt too, plenty of it. I felt uneasy after a large needless purchase. The rebellious jubilation that had accompanied big-buck outlays for totally unnecessary—or marginally necessary—books no longer packed a heavy punch. Self-examination and the concomitant guilt began to mark my bookstore forays. But that guilt was easily assuaged by the addictive mentality, the addictive cycle. Sure I felt guilty, but the guilt only prompted me to buy again because I knew that in buying again I would reap an ephemeral high, a high that would temporarily deaden my senses to the guilt, but which would also eventually throw me from its heights. And then I'd be bummed again. So I'd buy to ease that pain, and the cycle would begin all over again.

I embarked upon contingency buying, another of the diabolical manifestations of the disease. In contingency buying the idea is to purchase books in anticipation of future trends. That way when something hits big, you are already conversant on the topic—or at least you have a voluminous personal library dealing with it. This sort of knowledge plays big at social affairs and with other bookish types, where dropping *au courant* titles and authors scores points. How big could a prescient biblioholic have been in the late 1970s had he sported shelves of volumes on India before the subcontinent became all the rage? Or had he been able to anticipate the Frank McCourt industry and the infatuation with all things Irish in the 1990s? What if, the biblioholic worries, Upper Volta or Bhutan becomes the next rage, and he or she possesses no relevant books or knowledge about these countries? Who knows what literary figure from the past will throw off the integuments of obscurity and ascend to literary prominence? What if James Fenimore Cooper or Theodore Dreiser makes a posthumous comeback? And the biblioholic, without a single Natty Bumppo novel, or even *Sister Carrie*? Or, who will be the next Don DeLillo or Barbara Kingsolver? Biblioholic minds want to know.

I know it's weird—it may even be sick—but that is the kind of monomaniacal weirdness that takes control of a biblioholic's mind. That is the type of single-minded, obsessed, uncontrollable craving that torments a biblioholic's soul. No degree of duplicity is beyond the buying biblioholic. All manner of mental gymnastics and moral prestidigitation are fair game for the book fiend who wants to justify his or her purchases. I know. I have tried them all. I didn't need good reasons to buy books—any reason would do. I would go into a store to buy on Myanmar, Nepal, Mongolia, and Peru, trying to anticipate the next global hot spot. I wanted to survey the theological landscape, so I gobbled up all I could find on liberation theology, the Southern Baptist Convention, and lesbian nuns. If Jim Lehrer had discussed the Malaysian rubber crop one evening, I'd buy a book on it the next day. If Martin Amis delivered a speech on *Book TV* one Saturday evening, I'd be pulling his entire corpus off the fiction shelves as quickly as my arms would allow. I brought home two Emeril Lagasses and a Julia Child one day because I was hungry. Oh, I had no intention of reading such tomes. How could I? I was too busy buying them.

And, all the while, there was the shame, the guilt, the implacable inner voices: "You buy too much"; "You're hooked"; "Books control your life"; "You are a total, irresolute, pusillanimous, handwringing, prevaricating wuss!" And then I'd swear off of them. I would resolve to leave books alone, to live without them. And I would—for a while. But invariably one day I would think of the seductive tomes, the lurid and comforting environment of the bookstore, the handling and stroking of the volumes, the cradling of them in my bosom. Before I knew it, I was strolling from the store with sixty dollars' worth of books under my arm, momentarily satiated but knowing full well it was only a matter of days, maybe even hours, before I would need books again.

Bookstore clerks began to recognize me and titter into their hands when they saw me coming. They'd say things like "Boy, you sure read a lot" and "Only twenty-five today?" Others dispensed with the pleasantries and displayed their irritation. "Updike?" one said as I made inquiry at the desk. "We don't have any Updike. You have all our Updike."

Books were all around me at my apartment, settling in ever-growing stacks, pile upon pile. It began to affect my psyche, making me feel uncomfortable, claustrophobic, confused. It was a problem of such enormousness that even I, in my mentally diseased state, recognized it. Obviously, something was wrong. Something had to be done. So I sold my furniture, except for my rocking chair, and bought more books. That eased the angst—temporarily.

Friends began to shy away from me, refusing invitations they had previously eagerly accepted. "Hey, guys," I'd say, "let's go grab a quick one down at Barnes & Noble. What d'ya say?"

They'd look me up and down and say, "Friend, when's the last time you bought some clothes?"

Then it branched out into my love life, poisoning my relationship with the person I cared for. It came to a head one day when a fifty-three-pound white box arrived at my apartment while she was visiting. I told her it was the annual shipment of braunschweiger from Milwaukee. "I get one every year," I said. But, suspicious, she opened

21

it. It was the complete works of Charles Dickens, twenty-one volumes, hardbound and illustrated.

"More books," she said. "That's all you think about. Books!"

"But, honey," I said. "I love Dickens. You know that. And look at the design and the illustrations, the matching covers, the matching . . . Where are you going?"

She marched past me and into the kitchen, threading her way through a maze of book piles until she came to one which she unstacked to approximately mid-pile. "There's a *Pickwick Papers* here," she said, holding a volume. "You said you'd stop buying doubles."

(When she had first expressed concern over my book-buying some months previous, I had told her that the day I began to buy doubles without knowing about it was the day I would seek professional help. Since that day, she had spent much of her time in my apartment surreptitiously analyzing the titles in my stacks, searching, I supposed, for the telltale duplicates.)

"But that's a paperback," I said, smiling confidently.

"And so's this," she said, pulling the next volume off the stack. It was a different *Pickwick*.

"That's the Penguin, honey. The first one was a Signet Classic. I don't buy two of the same type," I said.

She stomped past me back to the living room and began feverishly picking up books from one stack, quickly assaying the titles, and slamming them onto another stack.

"Careful," I said. "You start a chain reaction and we both die." But she ignored me.

"Here's a *Little Dorrit*," she said, waving a Penguin volume. "How many of these do you have?"

"Only one," I said, smiling gratuitously.

"Here's another one," she said, waving another *Little Dorrit* with one hand while keeping her other hand behind her back. I noticed a sarcastic edge in her voice.

"Same deal, hon," I said. "Penguin and Signet Classic. Two different books entirely."

"So what's this *Little Dorrit* then?" she crowed triumphantly. It was another Signet Classic. I cleared my throat. "You lied to me!" she wailed.

"Two books," I said, putting on a treacly face. "Two identical *Little Dorrits*, that's all. I goofed. I screwed up. No big deal."

"I bet if I went poking around this place I'd find three, maybe four of those things." She looked at me hard.

"What? Because of one little honest mistake? Your imagination is out of control."

"No. You're the one who's out of control," she said. "Look at this place."

"C'mon," I said. "I can quit anytime I want to."

"Okay, send them back," she said. "Box them up and send them back—right now."

"Honey, they're hardback. I don't have the hardback set," I said. She seemed to melt slightly, so, thinking it a moment fraught with the potential for rapprochement, I snuggled up to her, offering her whispered blandishments and promises of my everlasting love. But instead of responding in kind, she focused her gaze on a stack of books immediately over my right shoulder.

I turned to look but was cut short by a horrific shriek. "What's this?" she screamed, throwing me away and violently knocking the top half of the tower to the ground. "Look, you spineless biblioholic. Look!"

Then I saw them mixed in the stack—in hardback, with covers, with illustrations. She picked them up one at a time, waved them in my face, and as she did so she screamed the title of the volume—*"Little Dorrit! Pickwick! Dombey! Bleak House! Edwin Drood!"*—before firing them down the slim parting of book piles that led to my bedroom. Then she turned her full fury on me. "You're a no-good, compulsive, addicted, out-of-control, lying, relationship-breaking, life-destroying book fiend! Pack them up right now, or I am out of here—for good!"

"What?" I said, trying to buy time. "Which ones?"

"Choose!" she wailed. "Dickens or me. Books or me."

I put my chin in my hand and began considering my options when she turned on me and screamed, "You love Dickens more than me!" She stormed out the door and stomped down the stairs.

I sprinted to the railing. "But I love you more than Trollope," I called after her, "more than . . . than *Anne* Brontë!" But to no avail. She stalked off unheeding.

I returned to my apartment and threw myself into my rocker and stewed. She didn't understand me. Nobody understood me.

That night the dreams started. They were always set in bookstores. I would be carrying too many books; huge books with legs would chase me, and I would run in slow-motion, dropping books, and crashing into things. One night I bolted upright in bed, overcome by the sensation that I was smothering. A coffee-table book, *Gauguin: A Retrospective*, lay open on my face. I hurled it to the floor and sat on the side of my bed, frightened, confused, tormented. What was going on? What was happening to me?

The next morning I was outside my favorite bookstore even before it opened. I was shaking, sweating. Just an hour, I thought. Just a short respite to calm myself, to silence the inner screaming. Six hours later I emerged from the place pushing a shopping cart, my voice lifted in ariatic ecstasy.

At home I sat on the floor, Fagin reincarnated amid my pile of purchases, grabbing volumes, reading titles, and restacking them with delirious glee in different piles. My day's purchases comprised a compendium of the recondite: *The Book of Tofu, If the River Was Whiskey, Billy Budd, 14,000 Things to Be Happy About, All I Ever Wanted to Know I Learned in Kindergarten, The Ants,* and a German-Turkish dictionary.

So what if I don't read them immediately? I thought. So what if some of them deal with esoterica? Some people buy toy trains. I buy books. That's all.

I hauled the stack into the other room, looking for space, and when I began moving piles around I came upon something disturbing: three Penguin *Billy Budds.* I didn't remember buying these. Must have been a three-for-one sale or something, I thought, rationalizing. I like books, sure, and I buy a lot of them, I'll admit it, but I'm in control. I always know what I'm doing. Me, a biblioholic? Nah.

I started poring through some of my stacks and found three copies of *Saint Maybe.* But I remembered them. One was a gift, another I bought at a garage sale for next to nothing, and the third was the original I had bought before acquiring the other two. I saw three copies of *Winesburg, Ohio.* Two had the same cover, but one I had loaned to some moron who used a piece of bacon for a bookmark, and the grease had spread throughout the book. I kept digging—*Lonesome Dove*— three copies as well, all the same design, but one I bought at a used bookstore, another was from a superstore's discount table, and the third was a Christmas gift. I could always find a reason, an excuse, an extenuating circumstance for the multiple copies. There was a logical explanation for every one.

Then things turned ominous. Doubles began to pop up that I could not explain. My long-since dormant conscience began its probing, pinching dirty work—why were there two identical sets of Leon Uris novels, strikingly duplicated on the shelf? Why all the Robert Ludlums—two and a half sets? What were all these Wagons West books doing here—there must have been fifty! Why did I have six copies of *The Client*?

I started sweating. But still, the process of denial had me in its grip. Certainly, it looked bad, like I had been out of control on occasion, but that type of thing can happen to anyone once in a while. It's the honest-to-goodness, mindless addicts, the people who don't remember what they buy, who fill up both arms at used bookstores, who buy without examination, who need a wheelbarrow to get a day's haul out to the car, who have no intention of reading the books they buy—those are the biblioholics, the hard-core problem buyers. Some people expend every dime of their savings in their insatiable quest for books. Me? I still had $300.00 in the bank. Ha! I'm no biblio. I just like to buy a book every once in a while.

Then I saw them—a row of white boxes stacked against the wall behind piles and piles of random, unsorted volumes. I rushed violently toward them, thrashing through the piles, and when I reached them I yanked down the top box and opened it up. I started hyperventilating. "No!" I screamed. It was another twenty-one-volume set of Dickens, hardbound and illustrated. I grabbed for another box, jerked it down, unfolded the top. Another Dickens. I pulled down a third. Dickens. They were all Dickens!

It hit me hard. I threw myself on the floor and rolled around in self-flagellatory penance, bringing stack upon stack of books down onto myself. I lashed out at my books, socking them, pounding on them, tossing them in the air and allowing them to rain down upon me. I hurled them at the walls, the windows, the ceiling. I began hitting myself in the head with one of my *National Geographic World Atlases* (I had four). Finally, close to exhaustion, I threw my head into my hands and bawled deliriously. I had been living a lie. I *did* have a problem. "I'm a bum," I sobbed. "A miserable, wretched, degraded, sodden bum."

Then I remember letting forth an unintelligible guttural cry from the depths of my being, a cry of bondage and ineffable pain. I remember careening off a wall, knocking down towers of books, stumbling on some steps, sprinting madcap and headlong into the night, but then the image darkens, the living nightmare fades.

They found me, I learned later, in the bargain books section of my favorite bookstore. I was cowering in a corner—not a pretty sight, I am told—clutching a volume of Melody Beattie and thinking myself a metamorphosed beetle. (Let the codependency mavens go to school on *that*.)

I had hit bottom. This was as low as I could go.

CHAPTER TWO

Anatomy of an Addiction

No subtle manager or broker ever saw through

a maze of financial embarrassments

half so quick as a poor book-buyer

sees his way clear

to pay for what he must have.

He promises with himself marvels of retrenchment;

he will eat less, or less costly viands,

that he may buy more food for the mind.

He will take an extra patch, and go on with his raiment another year,

and buy books instead of coats.

Yea, he will write books, that he may buy books!

The appetite is insatiable. Feeding does not satisfy it.

It rages by the fuel which is put upon it.[1]

YOU HAVE HEARD THE CRY FROM THE DARKNESS. You have listened to the disconsolate yowling from the tenebrous depths of my soul. And perhaps you feel inclined to offer up a plaint of your own, to wit: What—*another* addiction? Don't we have enough addictions to worry about—drugs, alcohol, nicotine, caffeine, gambling, eating, not eating, shopping, shoplifting, sex, chocolate, work, television watching, fitness, religion, and who knows what else—without having to worry about books too?

Is there not a more wholesome, more educational, more cathartic and enjoyable activity in all of life's experience than the reading and loving of books? Do books not represent learning and intellect and everything good and proper about society and life?

Well, if it means anything to you, I empathize wholeheartedly with your outrage. I, too, have passed through the crucible of denial. I, too, have rationalized away the dangers of this hideous condition with panegyric paeans to learning and knowledge and all that. I know where you're coming from. And you may vent your spleen in impunity, knowing that you have in me a comrade-in-mind. But you'll get over it. You must. And as you raise your awareness and submit to the requisite healing process, you will begin to view with perspicacity this menace called biblioholism, see the thing as it really is, do away with the illusions, and get on with your life.

After all, we must name the evils; we must elucidate their wily lures. This thing is real. It is dangerous. The sooner you face up to your helplessness before it, the better off you'll be. And if you don't, well, things could get rocky. You may find your life as an innocent book-lover rapidly transformed into a nightmare existence wherein your every hard-earned dollar is pumped out for pyramids of superfluous volumes, where books become the most important things in your life, and even friends and family, hygiene and physical appearance, take a backseat to the obsessive quest. And from there it is but a short step to locking books away in steel-lined rooms and burying them in your backyard and doling out major dollars for things like a lock of Shakespeare's hair, one of Ernest Hemingway's number two pencils, or beer mugs fashioned in the shape of Gertrude Stein's face (this being the celebrated "Stein stein").[2]

Thus it becomes paramount that we lay down some specifics of this insidious disease. What's it all about? How does it happen? And how can we tell if we've put our heinies on the slippery slide to degradation and infamy? We begin with the symptoms.

PHYSICAL SYMPTOMS

First and foremost of biblioholic symptoms is the degeneration of those organs most central to the act of reading: the eyes. We biblioholics remove those Fearless Fly glasses we wear and we can't tell a sunrise from the illuminated dial of our alarm clock. This is because biblioholics, by definition, read everywhere—while lying down without a reading light, in dark restaurants, amid the jouncing distractions of a city bus, by firelight while backpacking in the Sierras. Everywhere. We must read, and considerations like proper lighting are not sufficient to sway us from our passion. If we insisted on klieg lights every time we cracked a book open, we'd never get anything read. Torquato Tasso, a sixteenth-century writer, even enlisted the luster of his cat's eyes to help him see.[3] Not even failing eyesight could turn the great English diarist Sam Pepys from his all-possessing love. "So to bed," he wrote one day in 1668, "my eyes being very bad; and I know not how in the world to abstain from reading."[4] Fourteen months later he was blind.

And if blindness is not our destiny, then we pay with our looks. It happens to all of us. We latch onto a book we *really* want to read (like every other night or so), prop that thing up on our chests in bed, get totally absorbed in it, and the next thing we know our alarm clock is jangling and the window shades are bright with the morning sun—and we're still reading. One or two nights of such debauchery we can handle. But eventually our face will pay—in the form of saurian Jerry Tarkanian eyelids, eyeballs that look like IBM circuitry, and bags under our eyes the size of bowling balls. And what about the dread "browser's neck," the product of a continual rightward craning of the neck to read vertically stacked books on the shelf? Don't tell me that's pretty.

All of which are *above* the shoulders. Below deck, many of us are the proud owners of fannies that have spread to the size of the Mississippi Delta, the obvious physical fruit of a life spent in chairs. In fact, the metaphysical act of becoming sedentarily one with our favorite chair for hours upon hours, days upon days, may eventually result in the form of a far more troubling bodily symptom: atrophy. Many of us have the muscle tone of a twelve-year-old couch. Bibliophile Leigh Hunt tells of one Mrs. Benjamin West, who martyred her body to books, a physician declaring "that she lost the use of her limbs by sitting in-doors" reading.[5]

Proper hygiene may also be a casualty. While some biblioholics can put on the brave front, driving off the demons and pulling it all together every morning to assume at least a quasihuman demeanor, others of us throw the niceties of proper bearing to the wind. Part of this is because most of us have bought ourselves into poverty, and the price of even the most rudimentary toiletries—namely, soap, shampoo, etc.—is beyond our bankrolls. (Although those of us in the disease's later stages do save money on hair gel.)

But another part of it revolves around time. A shower can consume a full thirty minutes of prime and irreplaceable reading time, if shave and shampoo are figured into it. So we eschew the niceties. And we assume the demeanor of Apuleius, a prodigious writer and reader who, caught up in literary labor, allowed his hair to become "tangled, twisted and unkempt like a lump of tow, shaggy and irregular in length, so knotted and matted that the tangle [was] past the art of man to unravel."[6] Adrien Baillet was so into his books that he found time to go outside but once a week.[7] Another man, Carneades, was incapable of scraping up enough time even to cut his fingernails.[8]

LIVING ENVIRONMENT

A biblioholic's residence speaks volumes about his or her condition. Telltale signs are everywhere, not only where they may be expected— that is, in the bookcase—but in other locations as well, for really now, who has shelf space enough to accommodate the vast and ever-growing supply of books a biblioholic regularly takes in? There is, simply, never enough room. Thus, we merely pile them up—on the floor, on tables, by our bed, in the bathroom, anywhere and everywhere.

And then, we refuse to throw them away—not of our own free will, anyhow. This is a primary symptom of the disease. Every book carries with it the baggage of fond association, from the copy of *Green Eggs and Ham* that we heard read to us six million times while snugly tucked under our childhood covers to the *Principles of Sociology* text that we never read in college and aren't about to read now. They all stay.

This accounts, in large part, for our militant antipathy to moving. Moving is a big enough hassle for the nonbiblioholic. Think of what it is for one hooked on books. All that time gathering up all those thousands of books, finding enough cartons to pack them in, taping them up, jeopardizing our every casual friendship in order to inveigle a crew to haul those heavy boxes to a truck, getting somebody to haul them off the truck, remembering where they are to go, unpacking them, and stacking them up again. Who needs it? And what if the place we're moving into is *smaller* than the one we're vacating? Now, renting another apartment to store our books—*that* makes sense. But moving? Get real.

Another telltale sign of biblioholism is furniture. Look at a biblioholic's living quarters. If he or she has furniture—not all biblioholics do—one particular item will leap out and grab your attention: the biblioholic's reading chair. While couches, settees, and love seats may be sprinkled about the area—they all may even match—this chair will look like it was ripped off in a midnight raid on a Saint Vincent de Paul box. The armrests will be worn through. With the right light, you can comb your hair in the reflection off the cushions. The springs will be shot. And sit down in the thing and your fanny will bounce three feet off the floor. Fashion-conscious biblioholics will refurbish it every few years. But more esthetically sensitive addicts will allow it to remain in its original state. After all, there is a sanctity about the place. It is where communion between biblioholic and book takes place, and any monkeying around with the authenticity of that place is aesthetically unnerving.

QUALITY OF LIFE

The biblioholic's raison d'être is twofold: to get books and to read them. That is what makes living worthwhile. And as can be imagined, this can have a deleterious effect on the quality of our lives, the most apparent of which is that we are notoriously poor. There's no way around it. Certainly, some have prosperity foisted on them, some make their fortunes before succumbing to the disease, and others possess the persuasive power to beguile a spouse into supporting their bookish habits. But these are rare. In large part, our monomaniacal obsession for books catches up to us right quick. We overspend on books, our checkbook is rapidly attenuated, and we are quickly thrown into the gutter of impoverishment.

Tough choices face the biblioholic at every step of the way—like choosing between reading and eating, between buying new clothes and buying books, between a reasonable lifestyle and one of penurious but masochistic happiness lived out in the wallow of excess.

For it is true, biblioholics would rather read than eat, would rather buy books than buy clothes. George Gissing frequently laid out money for books that, even in his own mind, would have been more prudently spent on the necessities of life. Standing outside a bookseller's shop once, "torn by conflict of intellectual desire and bodily need," his stomach rising up in borborygmic revolt, the classic battle raged in his mind. Books or food? A "plate of meat and vegetables" and no book or a "dinner of bread and butter" *and* a book? Satisfying base, corporal needs or feeding the immortal mind? He "paced the pavement, fingering the coppers in [his] pocket, eyeing the stall, two appetites at combat within [him]," and then he did what any of us would have done if placed in his shoes: he bought the book.[9]

So it is with clothes. Needless to say, we don't evoke the *GQ* charisma. Nobody's going to liken our attire to that swinging down a Parisian runway. It's not that the fine points of fashion are beyond us, it's simply a matter of priorities. Part of this is due to the fact that we read while dressing, and while our eyes are on the tome in hand, they are not on our socks, shoes, shirts, and other articles of apparel. We never *intentionally* make a fashion statement.

The other part of it is strictly financial. What about those shoes we're wearing? Are we trying to bring home some major symbolic point, or are there other reasons we've worn the same earth shoes for two consecutive Earth Days—and all the non-Earth Days in between? And that shirt? Are we attempting to resurrect the 1960s with those double-knit, rainbow-colored, flowered jobs we wear, or is that what runs out of the closet in the morning when we call, "What shirt should I wear today?" And those bell-bottoms and dweeb-like skinny ties? Are we trying to prove something or what? I am an old hand at biblioholic dressing. Some of my underwear is older than most of the Brat Pack novelists. One French biblioholic, Gaullieur, wore the same suit for *twenty* years in order to save money for books.[10] Erasmus, the theologian, once wrote, "As soon as I get any money I shall buy books first, and then some clothes."[11]

THE LATER STAGES

Do not be fooled, fellow sufferers, biblioholism can be a happy disease. Lifted to rapturous heights with the purchase of thousands of books, lingering over the same while lolling in studied ease in our favorite chair, we exult in their presence as they accumulate on our shelves and floor. There's a lot to be said for it in its early stages. After all, we're probably getting smarter. We're broadening our horizons, expanding our purview, becoming all that we can be in an intellectual way. Why, with books we can tie one on fiercely and, not only will we not feel it in the morning, we'll feel *better* in the morning.

But that's early on, when the disease is in its incipient stages. As the disease runs its course, the trail of devastation it leaves in its wake can send our lives reeling. Its ravages can be irreversible. All it takes is one flight of ecstasy, one stimulating encounter with the agent of addiction, and that's all she wrote. Maybe it's bowing to the allure of an unneeded volume while roaming the bookstore stacks one day.

Maybe it's getting into that John Grisham thumb-wetter for a few beneficent hours of retreat from the harried life society requires us to lead. If we get locked into it and emerge with our hearts sprouting wings, then we endanger ourselves with the hook that is biblioholism.

For we will return to it whenever times get tough. It is a crucial element of the addictive process. Retreat. Escape. Indeed, one of the surest ways of determining if someone is biblioholic is to test his or her reaction to pressure. When the going gets tough, does the biblioholic get going? Or does he or she read? Or embark upon other bookish behavior? Do we react to domestic strife by retiring to the study or the library to read? Do we walk through the door at the end of a particularly tough workday with six or seven new books under our arm? Do normally routine tasks about the home—like mowing the lawn, vacuuming the carpets, conversing with spouse and children—become so onerous to us that we read instead?

If so, we who once considered ourselves mere casual bookophiles may soon find ourselves embroiled in a cyclic inferno of reaction. We flee to the refuge when tension descends on us, and yet the relief we find there is evanescent. The nagging nanny of shame makes its initial appearance in our book life and accuses us of reneging on our responsibilities. We seek to ease the pain in reading or book buying, and yet the guilt and shame we experience because of our very flight is of such potency that we require relief from that as well, to which end we again seek the healing waters of books.

As the cycle deepens and we biblioholics spin ever more vulnerably within its vortex, we begin to withdraw into ourselves. This is one of the reasons biblioholics have few friends. Oh certainly, much of this is due to an innocent forgetfulness on our part. We get wrapped up in the tome of the day, we forget to call friends we had previously agreed to call, we don't remember appointments, we don't return phone calls. Sometimes we'll even let the phone ring, and not always when we're at a "good part."

And as for dating, well, we can write courtship off altogether, the trouble with it being, of course, that in order to make it work, we must actually be bodily present with the person we are dating. That means dinner, movies, concerts, cocktails, museums, miniature golf, and all sorts of other activities, all of which consume precious time, and some of which even cost money. Normal people don't seem to get off on our idea of a perfect date: sitting on two couches some feet apart with two separate lamps shining into our laps, reading two different books.

We could take our date into a bookstore with us, but then our behavior, not books, becomes the topic of conversation. And when that happens, Cupid goes on walkabout. Because, chances are, we're going to do what we normally do in a bookstore: buy books. And whoever we drag to the bookstore with us is going to get in our face for what we consider very normal behavior. Questions like, "Are you going to read all those?" "You've got to have five thousand books at home and you're going to buy more?" "How come you can drop seventy bucks on books for yourself, but when you take me to Denny's we have to go dutch?" will come up, you can count on that. The fact is, whoever we take with us will think we're weird and abhorrent. We'd much rather go alone.

Not that we're not weird and abhorrent. We *are*. We just don't want to admit it. It becomes paramount for us to justify our behavior. As we do this, another process rears its ugly head. Innate good sense—stifled though it may be—still packs enough credibility to make plain to us certain undeniable truths: that people who can hardly walk around their apartment without crashing into a stack of books have somehow meandered from the mainstream of society; that someone who hasn't bought a new dress or pair of shoes for a year but has every edition and printing of *Mrs. Dalloway* ever published has somehow transcended normalcy. And yet we must defend such excessive behavior; we must rationalize it away.

Thus is born denial. Consider the following statements:

*   *   *

"My husband dared me to spend over $100.00 today. He said I didn't have the guts to make the family eat soyburgers for another month, and I had to take him up on it."

"You mean you wanted me to mow the lawn today? Well, why didn't you tell me? I was in the house all day, down behind the furnace, reading."

"But all one hundred of these books in this box I bought today are *out of print*, honey. They are *unavailable* to the common consumer. What was I supposed to do? Pass them up?"

"Problem? I don't have a problem! I just happen to own fifty thousand books, that's all. A problem? Me? Ha!"

*   *   *

Notice any similarity in the foregoing statements? Right. They're all examples of a carte-blanche rejection of reality. Biblioholics are loath to admit they have a problem. Either their obsession with buying and reading is somebody else's fault, they were thrown into circumstances that necessitated heavy reading or buying, or the problem simply does not exist. And all these excuses are made for the purpose of assuaging their pestering and carping guilt pangs.

But it doesn't work. In fact, denial plunges us ever deeper into the cycle of deception: we hurt all the more, yet we deny we have a problem. And our biblioholism only gets worse. We may experience grandiose and megalomanic feelings while on buying sprees. We get into those hallowed aisles and all we can think of is buy, buy, buy. Our reasons may become ever more tenuous: "I'd like to read this one." "What a great title." "That big one there will fit in perfectly with all my other big ones." "What a terrific cover." And all the while our ratio of books purchased to books read will climb higher and higher.

It is at this point that we may begin buying doubles. Oh, we don't do it consciously—although there is a school of thought that *does* do it consciously: the scholars and collectors of fine and rare books. But we'll deal with them later. We common-run biblioholics, when we begin buying doubles for no other reason than we were unaware we had bought the single, are out of control. We think we're buying them for the first time!

And then things turn weird. We begin to get downright sneaky in our bookish behavior. We start hiding our books. We lie about where we've been, where we're going, how much we've spent, and how many books we've bought. We blame others for our problems. We may start talking to ourselves more than usual. We may even start talking to our books. One Silvestre de Sacy used to cry, "O My darling books! . . . I do love you all!"[12] Eugene Field wrote, "When of a morning I awaken I cast my eyes about my room to see how fare my beloved treasures, and as I cry cheerily to them, 'Good-day to you, sweet friends!' how lovingly they beam upon me."[13]

By this point the biblioholic is in desperate need of help, having so helplessly lashed himself or herself to books that all other interests—family, work, hobbies—fall by the wayside. Only books quench the insatiable thirst—and then only momentarily. The biblioholic will progress even further into the pit of helplessness until he or she personally develops a will to recover. Whenever that occurs, whenever the despair is powerful enough to effect a legitimate cry for help—whenever the biblioholic hits bottom—then that biblioholic may begin to reverse his or her life.

But we're getting ahead of ourselves here. The cure will be taken up in the last chapter. Now, we want to know about you. How bad have you got the disease? Where are you on the slide to infamy? The next chapter will reveal all.

Biblioholism: Weakness or Disease?

You've heard the charges; you've seen the sneers. Indeed, it is commonplace that our nondiseased peers stand back in arrogant contempt and attempt to drown us in a flood of guilt. They trot out the standard lexicon of pejorative epithets for our excessive behavior. They label us sordid and feckless creatures, no-count derelicts who flee their problems for a self-made nirvana of reading and book-love. Slobs. Losers. Cadging parasites. Dissolute gutter-bums with all the self-control of elected officials voting to raise their own pay.

And, indeed, in our most candid and ingenuous moments, can we not mount the courage to ask ourselves: What sort of sap becomes addicted to books? They dangle no physical hook like alcohol or heroin. They promise no mind-bending Elysium like hallucinogenic drugs. They tempt us with no material rewards like shoplifting or gambling. Why, they don't even taste good. In some ways, we book addicts are like that crank down the block who has three million license plates in his garage.

And yet, the moral weakness explanation seems too easy. For there seem to be those among us who become so infatuated with books from our very first encounter—so compelled, so driven, so obsessed—that we clearly have no control over our buying. Is it we who are buying those books, or is it something inside of us crying, "Give me books! I need books!"? It is a question that drives to the very heart of wellness and self-image. How easy it is to lambaste the profligate bookaholic who sits in manic and mindless glee among twenty-five thousand volumes while loved ones go without food. And yet, does such an attitude help that maniac? Does it propel him or her down the path toward recovery?

Obviously, it is compassion that is needed, not fulmination. The truth is, we do not *become* biblioholic; we are *born* biblioholic. We are out-and-out crazy—in a clinical sense. This is the only loving way to approach it. Plus it is in full concordance with the Zeitgeist. It explains why some seem to be inexorably drawn to biblioholism from their very first positive experience with books. It allows biblioholics to relieve the debilitating false guilt that is laid upon them by offering a biological explanation for what otherwise would be categorized as moral failure. And it undercuts the stereotype of biblioholics as degenerates who have lost control of themselves when in the presence of books. And, besides, I'm a biblioholic too, and the last thing I want is some self-righteous tent-preacher type getting in my face about how I'm a weak-willed, spineless sinner, lost in the dregs of my own moral fecklessness. The case for biblioholism as an inbred, inherited disease bodes well for us biblioholics. It gets us off the hook.

Unfortunately, there is a problem in it, and that is, we can't prove a doggone thing. No one can get right down to the nitty-gritty and finger this chromosome or that DNA molecule as the villain. We can put men on the moon and microwave ovens in every kitchen, but when it comes to proffering scientific evidence to disable the emasculating incubus of guilt that hangs ominous and foreboding over our heads, the scientific community catches the first plane south. Why, it has yet to even *address* the problem.

Oh, sure, there is some circumstantial evidence, feeble though it be, that biblioholism is genetically transmitted. While history records no babies emerging from the womb with books in their hands, some youngsters have demonstrated biblioholic traits at startlingly early ages:

✳ ✳ ✳

Jonathan Swift could read any chapter in the Bible before he was three.[1]

Henry Bradshaw, at age three or four, had a library of five hundred books that included, not the works of some early-day Dr. Seuss or *Big Bird's Big Book*, but the *Odes* of Horace and other estimable tomes.[2]

The first word Edmund Gosse said was not "dada" or "mama" but "book."[3]

Frederic Myers, at age six, read Virgil in the Latin, albeit with the help of an interlinear translation.[4]

✳ ✳ ✳

Indeed, while it would seem that such precocity is genetic—and that book-madness may be inherited—we have in our society a wealth of skeptics who maintain that all this evidence proves is that these were some very smart little kids. We cannot afford such Neanderthalian benightedness, and our society cannot afford it. We biblioholics will never get healed if we have to come to grips with the prospect that it's our fault that we're out-of-control book fiends.

We need a full-fronted, no-holds-barred scientific inquiry into the origins of the disease. We need action, research, government grants. We need a book by Melody Beattie. On behalf of the entire biblioholic community, I exhort scientists everywhere, I adjure them, I fall to my knees in importunate supplication: find *something!* Don't let it be our fault!

CHAPTER THREE

Taking the Test:
Are You a Biblioholic?

To deny all is to confess all.[1]

IT'S OH SO EASY TO DETECT—the rapacious buying binges, the after-hours reading, the craven flight to the library whenever things get tough—so obvious to the eye, isn't it, *in somebody else?* But now we're going to turn the tables, folks. We're going to get personal. In this chapter, we're going to look at *you.*

So, clear off your reading desks, ratchet that 100-200-300 bulb up to the max, flick your BIC, top off that glass of Thunderbird, and get ready to let that visceral flush of guilt and pain do its purgative duty for once and for all. It's test time, people, time to trash all of those timeworn excuses, time to eighty-six all of those felicitous rationalizations that so readily await deployment on the tip of your tongue. Because we've heard them all, and they just won't cut it here.

Surprised? You shouldn't be. Every book ever written about addiction has a quiz section like the one you'll be taking shortly. Questions that probe the innermost recesses of your mind. Questions that, when you read them, make you feel like somebody's been watching every minute of your life for the past five years. And you can handle this thing any way you want to. You can even cheat. After all, you already know the right answers. You know what the test writer is trying to prove. You can plug in the answers that will test biblioholism-negative, lift up onto your toes, and prance out into the world in deluded and self-indulgent ignorance of your condition.

But, come on now, that's not going to help you. It's trite but true: cheat on tests like these and you only cheat yourself. But it's your life. You're the one with the book problem. Oh, don't kid yourself. You picked this book off the stands and you've made it to the third chapter. You can deny it all you want, but it just doesn't wash. *You* have a problem.

The real question is: How big of a problem? A neophyte, giddy with excitement at the prospect of cruising the aisles one Sunday afternoon a month, is looking at something altogether different than the person who gets the shakes when he or she forgets to tote a volume into a restaurant. But we demur. The first quiz requires yes and no answers. Be as honest as your stomach allows. The grading scale is at the end.

HOW BIG OF A PROBLEM? ? ? ? ? ?

1. When you go to a bookstore with a friend, are you usually carrying more books when you leave than your friend is?
2. Do you wake up the morning after, unable to remember how many books you bought or how much you spent on them?
3. Do you, inexplicably, yank down a volume from the store shelves, open it, and shove your nose deeply into the binding, hungrily inhaling the ink and paper smells?
4. Have you ever bought the same book twice without knowing it?

5. When you go to a bookstore after work, thus arriving home late at night, do you lie about where you have been, telling your spouse you were at a bar?
6. At Christmastime, do you buy your loved ones books that *you* want to read?
7. Have you ever given up on a book before you started it?
8. Are you unable to walk through a mall without stopping at a bookstore?
9. Do you have a personal library on an entire subject, none of which you have read?
10. Do you ever buy books simply because they were on sale?
11. Have you ever bought a book because you liked the cover design?
12. When at a garage sale, is the first thing you look at the books?
13. Have you ever been fired from a job, or reprimanded, for reading?
14. Have you and your immediate family ever "discussed" your book-buying and reading habits?
15. When you watch TV, do you always have a book in your lap for slow parts and commercials?
16. Do you "watch" television sports with the sound off?
17. Does panic set in when you find yourself in a barber's chair or at the salon with nothing to read?
18. Have you ever suddenly become deeply interested in an obscure topic and immediately bought six or more books on that topic?
19. Do you ever lie about how many books you've bought?
20. Do you devise grand and devious strategies for getting

your books into the house to avoid your spouse's or
family's scrutiny?

21. Has your book buying ever embarrassed your family or
friends?

22. When a stranger walks into your house or apartment, are
his or her first words usually a comment about your
books?

23. If someone asks you for a reading list of the twenty most
influential books you've ever read, do you happen to have
such a list *on your person?*

24. Do you have at least six books next to your bed?

25. When a bookstore clerk has been unable to locate a certain
book in the stacks, have you ever been able to find that book?

Count up the number of yes answers. If you answered yes to more
than four questions, you are looking down into the deep and woeful pit
of biblioholism. If you answered yes to more than eight, you are
hanging by your fingernails on the edge, your legs kicking in the empti-
ness and your eyes imploringly turned heavenward for rescue. And if
you answered yes to more than twelve questions, you are in space right
now, a full-throated scream careening off the canyon walls, and it's only
a matter of time until you splat onto the canyon floor with a puff of
dust and a hearty yelp à la Wile E. Coyote of cartoon fame. But then,
you already knew you were kind of weird.

In the next test we find out just *how* weird. Just exactly how far out
into the nothingness of the chasm of biblioholism have you fallen?
How bad have you got the book disease? Each question in this test
offers three possible answers. Please select only one. Again, honesty is
of the utmost. A grading scale follows.

* * *

1. You are playing host to an elegant dinner party for eight—four couples including you and your spouse. The food is delightful, the wine perfect, the setting congenial, the conversation scintillating. However, there is a lull: talk stops, eating slows. One of the party, to relieve her ennui, pulls from beneath her chair a book and dives deeply into it, oblivious of the proprieties of the occasion. Needless to say, this person's solecism captures the attention of all. As host, you feel you must do something. What do you do?

   a. Express your outrage at this unconscionable breach of social etiquette.

   b. Begin discoursing brilliantly on a topic of interest to all.

   c. Go to your shelves, pull down a dozen or two volumes, and hand one to each of the nonreading diners, while placing the rest of the books in the center of the table.

* * *

2. It is nigh unto sleeping time for you and your spouse. You are in bed and the reading light is on above your heads. Your spouse closes up his or her book, clicks off the light, and amorously snuggles to your side, promising to bestow upon you ardent connubial favors upon the disposal of your own volume. What do you do?

   a. Quickly lay your book aside and accede to the rigors of your spouse's amatory program.

   b. Agree to your spouse's demands this time, but insist on getting separate reading lights for the future.

c. Drive him or her away with an NBA-style rebounding elbow, flip the light back on, and return to your tome.

* * *

3. Your book buying has been halted by the barrier that eventually stops all book buying: lack of storage space. How do you react to this problem?
   a. You sell some of the books, or give them away.
   b. You jettison existing space-takers, like furniture and large appliances.
   c. You acquire additional space—that is, you buy or rent houses, build annexes, rent storage space.

* * *

4. What do you do when your friends wish to see your personal library?
   a. You tell them to "go for it" and leave them to their own devices.
   b. You get squeamish when you witness them handling your books, bending them and possibly creasing the bindings, and even setting their drinking utensils on them, but you allow them to continue unremonstrated.
   c. You allow no one to enter your library unless clothed in airtight suits similar to those worn on Gemini space missions, lest they track in any damaging foreign organisms, and then *you* alone handle the volumes.

*   *   *

5. When you give a book to a friend as a gift, what do you expect that person to do upon receipt of the volume?

   a. Thank you, put the book aside, and move on to other matters.

   b. Fall to his or her knees in profuse thanks and begin seriously reading the tome immediately, callously disregarding everything and everyone else present.

   c. Listen rapturously while you explain in detail the fine points of the particular volume—which may include the reading of excerpts—and how they specifically relate to the recipient, before digging into the reading of the tome right there.

*   *   *

6. You have just run out of gas or had car trouble on a deserted stretch of highway. Following your initial feelings of anger and disappointment, you realize that you may be there for some time. However, you also realize that you failed to bring any books with you. What do you do?

   a. Sit and stew and wait for help.

   b. Read the manuals and insurance policies in your glove box.

   c. This would never happen to you as you always have books with you.

*   *   *

7. You are driving your car with a number of newly purchased tomes in the passenger seat, all of which are unmarred and absolutely refulgent in quality. In the

backseat sits your spouse. You are:

a. Training to be a chauffeur.

b. A sexist of the first order.

c. A biblioholic merely exercising your priorities.

8. Your house has a dilapidated, fragile appearance because the rafters, beams, floors, and underlying joists sag dangerously. The slightest whiffle of a breeze could reduce it to a pyramid of firewood. You are aware of the problem. You blame:

a. The fifty thousand volumes you have lining every possible wall and occupying every possible inch of floor space.

b. The quality of wood used in the construction.

c. The obviously shoddy workmanship with which the house was erected.

*   *   *

For every answer "a" you selected, give yourself 5 points; for every "b" you selected, 10 points; and for every "c," 15 points. Tally up your score and match it with the following evaluation guideline:

40–59: Accept our sincere apologies. You are no biblioholic. Shop till you drop.

60–99: If you don't have a problem now, it's only a matter of time until you hear the voices and see the hideous little insects crawling up and down your arm.

100–120: You're gone. Further reading in this book may help you. But then again, it may not. Solicit intervention immediately.

CHAPTER FOUR

The History of the Book

Of making many books there is no end.

(Ecclesiastes 12:12, KJV)

SO, HOW DID IT ALL BEGIN? Whence came this omnipotent force that rules our lives and dominates our days? Are we the first generation that has bowed to the benumbing nostrums of self-help books? Is it our crowd alone who saw the genius of the celebrity bio? What about diet books? And physical fitness books? Are they genres peculiar to our century or did they see genesis in earlier eras? Is Gutenberg really at the fulcrum of history, or were there market forces at play even before the doughty German started rolling the presses?

Good questions all. And to better understand the book world—and our addiction to it—we must understand the history of the book. Many such histories have been written down through the ages, highlighting the milestones of publishing history. And interesting they have been. But the question must be broached: Did they really give us the straight poop? Did they tell the real, unexpurgated, unbowdlerized story?

Sadly, they did not. New information has come to the fore, information that offers at least partial explanation for the works and ways of publishing in these new days of another millennium. Thus, the *real* history of the book, never before offered to a book-crazed society:

🏛 10,000 B.C.

First gardening book, Adam's *Landscaping the Classic Mesopotamian Way: Highlighting That Unusual Tree,* published.

🏛 9999 B.C.

Eve, after brush with serpent, kicks off megamillion-dollar recovery-book industry with *Picking Yourself Up After the Fall.*

🏛 9995 B.C.

A Very Brief History of Time published; very brief, not only because of limited span of history at the time, but also because it was chiseled in stone. "There's got to be a better way," publishers moan in days leading up to inaugural Fertile Crescent Booksellers Association (FCBA) convention.

🏛 9991 B.C.

Tote bag invented; millions shipped to booksellers in anticipation of first FCBA convention.

🏛 9990 B.C.

At inaugural FCBA convention in Ur of the Chaldees, thousands of bookpeople ostensibly gather to brainstorm on practical problems in the industry, like publishing without paper, but instead devote entire time to parties, author breakfasts, keeping up with the giveaway demand, and debating whether to hold the next five thousand years of conventions in Hawaii or Cancun. However, publishers do put out a call for "integrity in the industry and people with vision to write books that the people out there want to read."

8000 B.C.

Megatrends 8000 published. Chapter titles include: "Caves No More: The Booming Housing Industry"; "The Emergence of Fire"; "The Age of Men"; "The Rise of the Fertile Crescent"; and "War and More War."

7871 B.C.

Euphrates Time-Life Publications kicks off its "The Way Things Work" stone-tablet series with *Earth*. Others to come include *Wind, Fire, Rain, The Wheel, Domestic Animals,* and *Drawing Those Weird Little Symbols on Cave Walls That Will Make Archaeologists 10,000 Years from Now Think We Had Culture.*

3600 B.C.

Unknown writer Methuselah cracks bestseller charts, despite low-profile ad campaign, with *The 900-Year Cholesterol Diet: It's Not What You Eat, It's How Long You Eat It.*

2990 B.C.

For seven-thousandth time in as many years, publishing world gathers at FCBA convention to bemoan state of publishing and issue impassioned call for "new vision." Following three months of brainstorming, paper, paperback books, huge advances, multibook deals, and author tours are invented.

📖 1200 B.C.
Highly publicized diet book published under title *Leviticus*. Sales flop. "Too many rules, too depressing, not enough variety, not enough attention to cholesterol," cry the critics. "And for crying out loud, give it a decent title."

📖 800 B.C.
Homer signs multibook deal, writes *The Iliad*. Sales sluggish, as it is an oral narrative and much of weighty content is lost in highly individualized translations.

📖 780 B.C.
Men Who Pillage, Loot, Lie, Deceive, Burn Towns, Decapitate People, and Catch Babies on Their Swords and the Women Who Love Them published in Assyria.

📖 750 B.C.
Homer writes *The Odyssey*. Acclaimed as "the new voice in literature; what the world's been waiting for—the Great Asia Minor Novel." Sales brisk. Book publishing industry gains fresh legs.

📖 749½ B.C.
Fifty-three authors sit down to write *Odyssey*-like epics, all claiming they can "do it better." Publishers, citing ruling credo of the day—that is, people want to read the same thing, only different—publish all fifty-three of them.

🏛 749 B.C.

The Odyssey reissued with full complement of *Odyssey* products—stationery, self-stick notes, gift books, calendars—to capitalize on primitive docudrama currently touring Asia Minor. (Paper edition published with Richard Chamberlain on cover.) Publishers unable to keep up with demand for *Odyssey* memorabilia.

🏛 748 B.C.

The Iliad reissued to tap wave of "Homer hysteria."

🏛 740 B.C.

Leviticus reissued under title *Eat Right or Die*, but sales still sluggish, limited only to an ethnic corner of the market.

🏛 736 B.C.

Fitness craze kicked off with revolutionary Spartan tome *Be Fit or Be Dead: The Spartan Workout Book*, endorsing toughening by exposure, near starvation, and daily flogging.

🏛 541 B.C.

The Crash of '39, prognosticating Medean takeover of Babylon, hits stands. Author executed immediately.

🏛 533 B.C.

Leviticus reissued as *Sinai Lite—Low-Fat, Low-Calorie, Low-Cholesterol, Low-Salt, Pork-Free Eating for People on the Move*, by Dr. Moses. Sales take off.

🏛 490 B.C.

Greek fitness craze continues as author Pheidippedes, midway through run to Athens to proclaim victory over Persians at Marathon, is struck by a "fantastic fitness concept"—*The "Nike Means Victory" Run till You Drop Aerobic Workout Book and Video*—which he dictates to relay runners along the way, completing it, just barely, before dropping dead.

🏛 350 B.C.

Plato's *Dialogues* appears. A humongous bomb with the general public, although lauded by critics.

🏛 349 B.C.

Cliffs Notes invented by Greek students because "nobody ought to actually have to read Plato's *Dialogues*."

🏛 335 B.C.

Aristotle's *Big Book of Athenian Lists* published.

🏛 320 B.C.

Plato's *Dialogues* reprinted as *Why Fat Guys Wear Tight Togas and Other Tough Questions*. Sales boom.

🏛 300 B.C.

Euclid writes *What Color Is Your Parabola?*, a revolutionary color-by-number approach to geometry written with the laity in mind.

241 B.C.

Instant historical account of Rome's first war with Carthage written, edited, published, and in the stores in *four* days. Sales damaged by typo on cover—book goes out as *The First Pubic War* instead of *The First Punic War*.

150 B.C.

Editorial and marketing departments at Back-to-Basics Books lock horns over release of Rosetta Stone, with editorial factions claiming major victory—book to be published at original length in original form (i.e., stone tablets). Sales suffer. "Book" is too large. Plus each copy weighs nearly a ton. Distribution network bogs down.

100 B.C.

Coffee table invented.

51 B.C.

Caesar conquers Gaul.

50½ B.C.

Six of Caesar's generals come out with instant celebrity bios: *Veni, Vici, Vidi*; *Vici, Veni, Vidi*; *Vidi, Vici, Veni*; *Vici, Vidi, Veni*; *Vino, Vino, Vino*; and *A Hitchhiker's Guide to the Rubicon and Beyond*.

50¼ B.C.

Profiles of generals appear in mass-market *Populi* magazine; generals also interviewed on "Bene Mane, Roma."

🏛 50 B.C.

Citing "healthy dynamic in-house tension," Back-to-Basics publisher Fay Rowe gives in to marketing forces at Cairo-based house. Rosetta Stone, although remaining in original form, is reissued simultaneously with complete line of Rosetta Stone products, a miniseries, cartoon show, breakfast cereal, action figures, and sixteen-copy floor display case. Six Back-to-Basics editors found thrust on their own blue styluses in house back room.

🏛 44 B.C.

After years of painstaking, laborious scholarship, Caesar biographer Publius P. Publius completes two-volume epic *Caesar: A Roman MacArthur.* Unfortunately, while book is in final galleys, Caesar is assassinated; book returned to Publius for a rewrite. Within days of murder, a slew of instant histories glut the market.

🏛 43 B.C.

Brutus cops million denarii advance to write his side of Caesar slaying, with working title of *Et Me, Caesar.*

🏛 26 B.C.

After years of sorting through ever-growing mounds of research, Publius's long-awaited *Caesar: A Roman MacArthur* is finally released, albeit to a tepid public. "We're Caesared out," one local critic wailed.

4 A.D.

Rosetta Stone reissued as book coffee table vis-à-vis a coffee-table book, with chess board and Trivial Pursuit pattern sculpted into top. Sales slow.

14 A.D.

Emperor Augustus nationalizes tax collection simultaneously with release of 3,200-page government instructional "booklet." Publishing world chimes in with no less than twenty do-it-yourself tax guides.

101 A.D.

Sixteen-book floor display of Rosetta Stone falls on unwary shopper in Cairo supermarket. Back-to-Basics recalls all copies of "book" to avoid mass litigation.

144 A.D.

Ptolemy publishes *Why the Sun Comes Up in the Morning and Other Imponderables of Every Day.*

285 A.D.

Men Who Love Men and the Women Who Hate Them published in Rome.

400 A.D.

Due to marketing foul-up, *Confessions of St. Augustine* issued as romance genre book.

📖 445 A.D.

Meat Is Murder, a proto-animal-rights polemic, published by Mort the Sensitive Hun in an effort to raise the consciousness of a barbaric horde. Attila counters with prophetic rebuttal, *Mort Is Meat*, which turns out to come true minutes after book hits stands.

📖 476–1350 A.D.

Middle Ages. Contrary to popular opinion, this near-millennium of history was not swallowed in a black hole of unenlightened yahooism. Books continued to be published, traditions in the trade continued to be revered. Despite deprivation, plague, government inquisition, and torture, the industry endured. Some of the more remarkable book events of those years included:

The Jousting Abstract. Sports books continue to sell, especially those heavy on statistics. Chain-mail piercings, death-infliction average, and direct-lance hits to joust ratio are only some of the stats highlighted in this particular bestseller.

A Crusader's Guide to Day-Care in Central Europe. Travel books go practical, offering the family that wants to crusade together a chance to drop the kids off before getting it on with the local infidels.

Trouble erupts on international *I, Genghis* author tour. At a signing in Samarkand, the celebrated Mongol leapt unprovoked to his feet, screamed, "Enough of the wine and cheese. We drink blood!" quickly slew fifty fans seeking autographs, and sacked the city, thus putting a stop to author tours for six centuries.

The Frugal Gourmet Cooks Gruel—but doesn't eat it. Even the Frugal Gourmet has limits. The culture of cuisine hits low-water mark during the Dark Ages.

Pardon Me, Sir, Would You Hold Still While I Impale You on This Spike? and Other Tales from a Chivalric Age published. Chivalry wasn't dead in the Dark Ages—in fact, it was born then. There was a right way for everything; etiquette books popped up everywhere.

Self-help books take a turn toward pessimism with Sisyphus Books' *Tough People Never Last, But Tough Times Do; When the Going Gets Tough, the Tough Get Tortured;* and *The One-Minute Executioner* leading the charts.

Humor books are rare, the only real money-makers being *The Teutonic Plague,* a French classic, and *Garfield Gets the Buboes.*

Rats!, a coffee-table book on the Black Plague, published. This bestseller featured some breathtaking photography.

🏛 1455 A.D.
Gutenberg invents printing press.

📚 1530 A.D.

Calvin and Zwingli, a cartoon book about a kid and his pet tiger, published but falls flat.

📚 1535 A.D.

Anne Boleyn's *Heavy, Megalomanic Monarchs Who Love Gluttony and Promiscuous Sexuality and the Women Who Love Them* published.

📚 1536 A.D.

Anne Boleyn beheaded by heavy, megalomanic monarch who loved gluttony and promiscuous sexuality and who also happened to be her husband, the king.

📚 1564 A.D.

Shakespeare born, lives life in obscurity as Stratford-upon-Avon barrel-stave maker and romantic who dabbles in occasional verse and watches a lot of plays in his spare time, but who is known chiefly because of high-collared shirts he wears.

📚 1588 A.D.

Battle of Spanish Armada breaks out as Spanish publisher, outraged because it is assigned inferior booth position at Frankfurt Book Fair for second year in row—"over in the corner, about halfway into the ladies' can"—dispatches fleet against British counterparts, who "always get the cherry spots."

🏛 1595 A.D.

Frankie Bacon, Sr., writes numerous manuscripts of plays—*Romeo and Juliet, Othello, King Lear*, etcetera—and stores them in his attic because he's too insecure to let anybody see them.

🏛 1620 A.D.

Frankie Bacon's son, Francis, a local critic and writer who at age four had dedicated his life to making his old man pay for naming him Francis, finds manuscripts of dad's plays in attic. He reads them and declares, "This is great stuff." But then, inspired by a popular international intrigue novel of the day (*The First Folio Fallacy* by Robert Doldrum), he metes out fiendish revenge by changing all the *s*'s to *f*'s and magic markering a line portrait of a goateed old barrel-stave maker he knows onto the frontispiece of all the manuscripts.

🏛 1763 A.D.

Colonists dressed up as English gardeners throw English horticulture books into Boston Harbor because, in words of revolutionary Sam Adams, "none of that bonny England stuff works over here. The nights are too hot and there's not enough rainfall." Revolutionary war begins.

🏛 1946 A.D.

Gandhi Diet published.

🏛 1964 A.D.

Pro wrestler Yukon Eric's *Hug Therapy* published.

The History of the Book

📖 **1970 A.D.**

Obscure academician encounters a text in a dark alley and the text deconstructs him with steel-studded Cliffs Notes. A call from ivory tower insiders to deconstruct all known texts becomes watchword of serious literature.

📖 **1977 A.D.**

Psychology book of year *Skinny, Balding Men with Beer Guts and Caterpillar Hats Who Watch Tractor Pulls on Television and the Women Who Love Them* published.

📖 **1988 A.D.**

Aisles widened at annual ABA convention to accommodate U-Haul trailers, as volume of giveaways increases dramatically.

📖 **1989 A.D.**

Sixteen-city book tour to promote celebrity's autobiography falls flat as celeb fails to read his own book first.

Thus far the recorded past. And what does the future hold? Look for these releases in the year 2010:

Martha Stewart continues to pump out the sellers, but also expands her areas of expertise with *Martha Stewart Solves the Middle East Crisis*—the problem was apparently the name plates at the conference tables; they were *tacky*—and *Martha Stewart Invents a New World Religion*.

Mars and Venus Travel to Mars and Venus, Respectively. And take John Gray with them.

The Chicken Soup series tries to find its roots with *Chicken Soup for the Stomach*.

Building on the success of *Monica's Story*, the now-famous presidential inamorata pens an ode to the former First Soulmate by the title *Leaves of Cigars*

Dave Barry's Autobiography of Dave Barry. It had to come eventually.

So great is the demand for idiots' guides and dummies' books that two new series are launched, each with hundreds of titles: the *How Dumb Can You Get?* books and the *C'mon, You're Dumber Than That* series.

And what about fiction? What will be streaming from our leading writers' pens ten years hence? Try these events on for size:

It's official. Five sentences putatively in the hand of the late author Ernest Hemingway were found on three yellowed bar napkins in a back room of Sloppy Joe's, a Key West bistro formerly patronized by the great American writer, and were immediately "expanded" into a novel, thus pushing the Papa's posthumous output beyond his "humous" one.

Biblioholism: The Literary Addiction

A computer joins the ranks of high-tech suspense writers. Under the pseudonym A.I., the computer pens a best-selling tale by the title of *Michael Crichton*.

After spinning mega-selling tales about a killer car, rabid family pets, and dead pseudonyms on a rampage, the most-read author in America, Stephen King, gets really weird with . . . oh, heck, I have no clue. One of his recent books featured a demon-possessed *plant*.

Speaking of the weird and wild, look for John Grisham to write a novel sometime in this decade that has no lawyers.

There will be a seven-volume set of novels that will be the biggest thing to hit the fiction world in decades. Will it be a new printing of *Remembrance of Things Past* or the complete Harry Potter series? Pick only one.

Oprah's Book Club goes in a radical new direction, as the queen of multimedia chooses a novel for her devoted fans that features a male who is not evil, but good. Sure, he gets killed on page 22, but still.

Building on this brief chronology, we now turn to our ancestors in disease—to see how they played out their obsession. For we are not the first in history to feel the magnetic pull of the printed word. Others before us have sunk just as low, if not lower, into the whirlpool of biblioholism. We begin with bibliomaniacs and bibliophiles.

CHAPTER FIVE

Bibliomaniacs and Bibliophiles

The bibliophile knows how to choose his books,

adding book to book after

having submitted them to various tests.

The bibliomaniac piles them up, one on top of the other,

sometimes without looking at them.

The bibliophile appreciates the book,

while the bibliomaniac weighs or measures it.[1]

BECAUSE OF ITS LACK OF EXPOSURE IN RECENT YEARS, biblioholism may seem like a relatively new addiction to some—just another fetish to line up with chocolate, work, shopping, or any of the other crippling behaviors that send the people of our day slouching couchward. However, biblioholism is no recent discovery; it is as ancient as the things to which its addicts have succumbed—namely, books.

But it was called by another name during the profligate years of centuries past. In fact, historically, two terms have been employed to differentiate between bookish behaviors: *bibliophilia* (book-love) and *bibliomania* (book-madness). The distinction between the two generally divides on the basis of motivation. A bibliomaniac is out to acquire and possess books, whereas a bibliophile, while not averse to possession, wants more to acquire the knowledge and wisdom contained therein.

In some cases the distinction is merely one of degree, with bibliomaniacs being those whose bibliophilia has run amok. They may have begun hoarding books with the intention of reading them at some indeterminate future time—like the *War and Peace* we have purchased with the hopes of eventually getting to—and ended up liking the feeling so much they hoarded for the sake of hoarding books. They allowed love of books and reading to grow until the yearning could only be assuaged by possession on a grand scale. The strength of their libraries was measured in numbers alone. They were seriously into quantity.

Consider the awe-inspiring French collector Boulard, an eighteenth-century Parisian lawyer who fell to manic book buying, stacking purchases on shelves, piling them up in closets, scattering them everywhere in his study until, the mass accumulation becoming so onerous, he allowed them to overtake every room in his house. He subsequently purchased six additional houses to store the burgeoning collection. Books were piled from first floor to attic. Walking amid the stacks sent them into threatening oscillations that could have, in an instant, buried the unwary visitor in an avalanche of books. "After being put into the library a volume was as lost as if it had been thrown into the bottom of the ocean," wrote Theodore Koch of Boulard's immense stash. When he died, Boulard had amassed from six hundred thousand to eight hundred thousand volumes. The sale lasted five years and market values were cut in half because of the glut.[2]

Others have been, if less prolific, equally as maniacal in their bibliomania. La Bruyère told of visiting a book collector and almost fainting from the smell of the black morocco leather in which the man's voluminous library was bound—a library into which he stepped only to show his collection to visitors.[3]

The problem with Boulard and other wild and crazy bookaholics of those years is that they didn't read the books they acquired. They simply bought them, and fueled by the attendant euphoria, they bought more.

In antipodal opposition to these acquisitive types is the white knight of the ancient book world: the bibliophile—the pure of heart and spirit, the lover of books for their contents. Whereas bibliomaniacs amassed books, piling them higher and higher, determining their import only by weight and measurement and exterior qualities, bibliophiles chose carefully which books to buy and then pored over them, appreciating them for their inner beauty and wisdom. While bibliomaniacs loved books for their outward appearance, bibliophiles loved them for what was written inside. For bibliomaniacs books were treasures to be protected, museum pieces, curiosities; for bibliophiles they were friends to be enjoyed. Bibliomaniacs bought voluminously and at random, or they mounted up on an acquisitive quest for rarities; bibliophiles subjected their acquisitions to heavy emotional quality control—they had to like the author, the subject matter, or some other aspect of the book before they bought it.

As can be expected, much acrimony exists between the two. Bibliophiles can say little good of those who acquire books solely as collectibles, and the invective in the past has risen to the heights of dudgeon. The rap, of course, is that intelligent, sensitive bookpeople *read* the books they buy. And, indeed, some of the great bibliomaniacs have lived in profound ignorance of the information contained in the volumes of their collection. One, a certain Count d'Estrees, was said never to have read at all, but to have piled away fifty-two thousand volumes. Another, a collector of books on astronomy, knew nothing of the science and refused to read his books or lend them out to others.[4]

And what of the incomparable Boulard? He had no idea what books he had. When Charles Nodier, who patterned the protagonist of his story "The Bibliomaniac" on the wild Boulard, asked Boulard for a certain book, the Frenchman walked from house to house, striking the walls and the floor-to-ceiling stacks of books and saying sardonically, "It is either here or there."[5] Boulard was a man unequivocally into quantity.

Not everything is so black and white, however. Some ancient bookaholics amassed great stores of books and read them too. One such notable was Richard Heber, a nineteenth-century English biblioholic. When he saw a book, it was his. He bought books of all kinds, in all ways, in all places. Buying duplicates and even triplicates was his distinct proclivity. His collection, like Boulard's, spilled out of his house, and he added seven additional abodes to accommodate his 200,000- to 300,000-volume stash, a total of two in London and six throughout England and the Continent.[6]

The great bibliomaniac Thomas Frognall Dibdin, who wrote a nineteenth-century dissertation on book-madness, was given the opportunity of viewing, upon Heber's passing, what no one during Heber's lifetime had been privileged to see: the sanctum sanctorum, namely, Heber's house. "I looked round me with amazement," Dibdin wrote. "I had never seen rooms, cupboards, passages, and corridors, so choked, so suffocated with books. Treble rows were here, double rows were there. . . . Up to the very ceiling the piles of volumes extended; while the floor was strewn with them, in loose and numerous heaps."[7] And that was in one of his eight repositories. But—and this is what muddies the waters—Heber also read his books. History shows him reading and studying right up until his death.

So, what are we to make of it? If one man can possess two hundred or three hundred thousand books and still be well within the suburbs of sanity, and the other can fill eight houses with books he never even read or looked at, how does that help us plot our coordinates on the continuum of biblioholism?

The crucial question for today's bookaholic—the litmus test—thus becomes: How many of the books in our libraries do we read? How many do we actually apply our eyeballs to in a cognitively meaningful fashion? For, after all, to lay claim to even a scintilla of sanity, don't we at least have to read some of the books we buy? The acquisition to reading index—is this not the gravamen? Where does the demarcation between "mania" and "philia" fall? What didactic criterion do we employ to separate the two? Eighty percent of books purchased read? Sixty percent? Twenty? Where does the line fall?

These are questions only we—each of us individually—can answer. How many of those old classics we bought ages ago, intending to read but never getting around to, take up space on our shelves? How many "message" gifts have we received from loved ones—books like *What Every Woman Should Know About Men, How to Stop Worrying and Start Living,* and *Thin Thighs in 30 Days,* which people gave us hoping we would read them and change our lives—have we hung on to when the prudent and expedient recourse would have been to dump them the moment they hit our hands? How many times have we stood gazing at our shelves and thought, "I've got to get rid of some of these books," and then never summoned the wherewithal to act on our thoughts? Are we, too, hovering dangerously close to Boulard-like infatuation?

Bibliomaniacs and Bibliophiles

These are serious concerns. For from infatuation, the biblioholic's path goes nowhere but down. Outright craziness sets in—the demented bibliotaphy (hoarding and burying books), the outrageous bibliophagism (eating books), the savage biblioclasm (destroying books), and a myriad of other manifestations of the eldritch.

But first, we must consider collectomania, the closest near relative to out-and-out bibliomania in today's world.

CHAPTER SIX

Collectomania

He is an universal Scholar, so far as the
Title-page of all Authors, knows the Manuscripts
in which they were discovered,
the Editions through which they have passed, . . .
He has a greater esteem for Aldus and Elzevir,
than for Virgil and Horace. . . .
[H]e cries up the goodness of the Paper,
extols the diligence of the Corrector, and is transported
with the beauty of the Letter. This he looks upon to be
sound Learning, and substantial Criticism.[1]

IT STARTS WITH SNOOPY DOLLS OR TEDDY BEARS and moves on to bottle caps, marbles, action Rambo figures, and butterflies, and then up to coins and stamps and insects, and finally, at its maturity, it tops out in something valuable and rewarding, something for which joy and satisfaction serve as concomitant pleasures for every new acquisition. No, not lawn flamingos or velveteen Elvis art. Books.

Collecting. It's an urge almost indigenous to the human species. At some point along the line, it will manifest itself in all of our lives.

Collectomania

I started with marbles. A whole big jewelry box of them—cat's eyes, steelies, boulders, cat's-eye boulders. But kids didn't shoot marbles in my boyhood neighborhood. Shooting marbles was the stuff of wily street urchins who lived by their wits and walked the streets of the big city. And I was a child of the suburbs. I didn't do anything with my marbles. They just kind of sat in the jewelry box. And every once in a while I would seek to legitimate their existence by overturning the box on the top of our linoleum stairs and watching them with glee as they thundered to the bottom like a thousand superballs let loose in a phone booth. But my mother objected.

So I turned to coins. Collecting coins is a great hobby. Sorting through rolls of coins from the bank, sticking them into little triptych books, rolling the coins back up, trotting back to the bank for more—it has all the elements of intense and moving drama. I did all that and more. And then, in the hobby's climactic moment, I got out my collection and "worked on" it—that is, I would get it out and *look* at it. As Dave Barry opined about the exciting hobby of philately: "Have I left any moments of drama out of this action sequence?"[2]

After that I got into maps. In those days road maps were provided free at the largess of the major oil companies. I had about five hundred of them. Oh, those thousands of happy hours, spreading my maps on the floor, finding maps of contiguous states with identical scales of miles, putting them together and then "driving" my little toy cars around on them. It was perhaps my favorite hobby of all. Then my dad said to me one day, "Why don't you go get a date for the prom like the other boys your age?" and I put away childish things.

It would probably be apposite of me to now chronicle my ascension from such humble beginnings to the true hobby of sages—book collecting. But to say such would be to lie. I love books, all right. My every ganglion pulses with desire when I see them. But I'm not a collector per se. I'm not into old and rare treasures. Incunabula. First editions. Gutenberg Bibles. Elizabethan novels in their original boards, uncut and unopened. The very copy of *Sophocles* that went down with Percy Shelley during his final fateful dip in the Bay of Spezia. That sort of thing.

It takes a special breed of person to collect books. Urbane and astute. Street-smart and book-smart. Willing to mix the bartering skills of the Istanbul bazaar with the erudition of professional acumen. Willing to undergo dire deprivation and enormous sacrifice simply to get their hands on a given book. Paying almost any price to obtain that hunted tome, to stack it up with the previous conquests, and then to exult in its existence. They are Indiana Joneses with Elzevirometers and price guides. In many ways collectors are a cut above the pedestrian bookaholic, the crème de la crème. They are the aristocrats of the book world, and no one can begrudge them their status.

However, collectomaniacs do have their ways, to put it diplomatically. As an alien to this close coterie of biblioholics, not subject to its arcane and mysterious pull, I have an advantage. I can stand back and observe objectively the works and ways of these very special biblioholics. For it is detachment alone that has allowed bookaholics of time past to draw their flaming arrows on the collecting world. Once one is bitten by the collecting bug, all objectivity is lost. Only outsiders have eyes that see and ears that hear. Only outsiders can see the fallacy of rarity for rarity's sake. Only outsiders can understand the futility of adding another first-edition *Moby Dick* to a collection of 115 previously acquired first-edition *Moby Dicks*. Only outsiders will see the humor in the story of one Frederick Locker-Lampson, who returned to a bookbinder a specimen of the man's handiwork with the complaint that the book would not close properly. The bookbinder surveyed the tome and pronounced his verdict: "Why bless me, sir," he said. "You've been reading it!"[3] An outsider can speak the truth. Because, face it, it's not going to come from the lips of somebody with 115 *Moby Dicks* locked away in some basement safe.

But enough. Collectomaniacs can be a very touchy group, and it is from the high moral ground of objectivity that we want to view this mania. So, let's get on with it. Let us then take a good, hard look at collectomania by delineating its criteria, the standards of collectomania.

RARITY

The *sine qua non* of collectomania is rarity. If everybody in the Western world has a copy of a given book, then obviously, the collectomaniac doesn't want it. You don't see collectors gathering about themselves, say, fresh, mint-condition copies of the forty-fourth impression of *Lord of the Flies.*

No, to collectomaniacs a rare book is one where only about one hundred copies were printed. Now, let's think about this for a moment. Why would only one hundred copies of a book be published? It must be an el crappo book, right? No sense publishing ten thousand copies of a book only the author and his or her immediate family will want, right? And yet collectomaniacs crawl all over each other for these rare books like preteen girls storming the gates at a boy band's concert.

But, if we burrow our way into the collector's mentality, it does make sense in a demented sort of way. After all, if they aren't going to read them, what difference does it make if they're lousy books? They're rare—that's the essence. Either that, or some ulterior motive is at play.

Limited editions of only a few score or a few hundred are often published by authors for friends and relatives, after which a regular pressrun in the thousands or tens of thousands is completed. But here again, why publish only a few books of what will doubtless be a popular book if not to capitalize on the mania for rarity?

Biblioholics of time past have even been known to artificially attenuate the supply of a given book. One Captain Douglas once purchased several hundred copies of a book called *Points of Humour* and then made a bonfire of them, destroying all but three, which he retained and which, he hoped, would soar in value.[4] Thomas Frognall Dibdin, the nineteenth-century chronicler of bibliomania, threw a huge bash once at which he put the torch to the many wooden blocks used as plates to illustrate his *Bibliographical Decameron*, thus making a reprint impossible.[5]

This mania for rarity is analogous to our society's infatuation with celebrity. Some celebrities are celebrities simply because they're well known; they're famous because they're famous. And rare books are oftentimes rare only because they're rare. Which brings up a question all discerning book-lovers should consider: What really, when you get right down to it, is the difference between Ed McMahon and a rare book? A troubling thought indeed.

CONDITION

Collectomaniacs are obsessed with the condition of their books and consume an inordinate amount of time speaking, in their recondite lexicon, of whether the book is poor, worn, fair, good, fine, foxed, rubbed, scuffed, bumped but internally fine, and so forth.

But in reality, most of these books collectomaniacs pine so after are pretty darn ugly in any normal person's eyes. The bindings are all faded, the lettering is sometimes rubbed off, the cover is shot. Why, most of those old suckers don't even have dust jackets! And hard to read! There's more margin than there is text, the spellings are weird, all the s's look like ƒ's, the punctuation is inscrutable, they fill up the first letter of every chapter with more curlicues than a mushy greeting card, and if that's not enough, the paper is *breakable*.

This is because most of these very valuable books are extremely old. Which calls to mind a story Mark Twain told in *The Innocents Abroad*. Twain's traveling party was touring the great cities of Italy under the guidance of a dragoman they called—as they called all of their guides—Ferguson. In Rome, Ferguson showed them the sights and, while guiding Twain's party through the impressive Vatican museums, he grew frustrated at their lack of response. Twain and Company were not comporting themselves like tourists. Their jaws weren't hanging in awe, their heads weren't shaking in wonder, and this bothered Ferguson. So he played his trump card—he showed them an Egyptian mummy. "See, genteelmen! Mummy! Mummy!" Ferguson rhapsodized. But Twain's party remained unimpressed, much to Ferguson's chagrin. After some preliminary inquiries about the mummy's name, one of Twain's group, the doctor, finally drove to the nub of the matter. "Mummy-mummy," he said. "How calm he is—how self-possessed. Is, ah—is he dead?" "Oh, *sacrebleu*," Ferguson responded, "been dead three thousan' year!" The doctor wheeled in fury. "Here, now, what do you mean by such conduct as this!" he said. "Trying to impose your vile secondhand carcasses on us! Thunder and lightning, I've got a notion to—to—if you've got a nice *fresh* corpse, fetch him out!"[6]

Can we not learn a thing or two from this enlightened doctor? Collectomaniacs are forever rhapsodizing about books in their "original condition." Put two copies of the same book on a table, and the uglier of the two will fetch the higher price. But, really now, let's look at this objectively. If we want to read the Bible, we don't have to read the exact same Bible Gutenberg read. We don't have to grub around Europe all our lives to find some old, ugly book that we'll encase in glass like an icon once we find it. Millions of Bibles are printed every year. In nice bindings that look halfway decent, with pretty covers, and in English too. And we can actually read them if we want to!

One other note on condition—the matter of "unopened" pages. Collectors salivate over books that have not yet had the actual pages separated from each other. They're stuck together on the foreedge. Not to put too fine a point on it, but, not only have these books never been read, THEY'VE NEVER EVEN BEEN OPENED!!! I ask you, does this make sense? We can at least *read* baseball cards.

FIRST EDITIONS

First editions are an absolute passion in the collectomaniac community. How better to drive right to authors' creative works in their original form, how better to get close to the authors, to achieve a sort of metaphysical oneness with their thoughts as they first presented their work to the public, than to possess a first edition?

A.S.W. Rosenbach said it thusly: "A first edition is almost as much the original work of its author as the painting is of an artist. I suppose there are people . . . who would just as soon have an edition of Keats's *Poems*, for example, well printed on good paper, in a handsome modern binding, as a first edition in its original boards! I only hope I shall never meet them."[7]

This is all well and good. We can't begrudge someone seeking this sort of mystical nexus with the creative process. And yet there's a big problem with first editions: you have to go to code-busting school just to figure out what is and what isn't a first edition. You'd think because they knew first editions were such a collector's item that publishers would make a big deal about it. Maybe even put it on the cover in seventy-two-point type or something. But no. The industry makes a Chinese puzzle of it. Each publisher has its own identification marking—from the bold, forthright words "First Edition" on the copyright page to cryptic combinations of widely dispersed and inscrutable symbols: code letters on the copyright pages, little letters on the rear cover, Roman numerals following the last line of text on the last page, a date on this page, different colors on that page. Some don't even indicate it at all.

In fact, it is a mark of enormous distinction among collectomaniacs to be able to identify a first edition *all by their lonesome*. Like male drivers lost in a strange city, they never want to—heaven forbid—ask somebody. That's why collectors are always whipping little guidebooks out of their pockets—they're checking on first editions.

AUTOGRAPHED, INSCRIBED, AND DEDICATED COPIES

These are very hot items among collectomaniacs. An author's signature on the flyleaf of his or her book; an inscription from one person to another; an autographed copy of a book presented to the person it was dedicated to—signatures and inscriptions can add presence and stature to a book; they can enhance a book's value.

But this area is a little tricky, for it depends on who is doing the inscribing. If you happen to write, "Could stand a rewrite, especially Part III," on the flyleaf of your first-edition *Tender Is the Night*, you can pretty well be certain that your copy is not going to increase in value. But if Hemingway wrote it, you'll want to buy a glass case and hire a battalion of rent-a-cops to protect it. For that inscription tells you something about Hemingway; it gives you insight into the machinations of his mind—especially if he drew smiley faces over his i's.

As a noncollecting biblioholic, I can see the fuss, up to a point. We must take a harder look at the autograph and inscription question, however. And here again we go to that paragon of perspicacity: Mark Twain. Although some of his notions may have been "stretchers" practicality-wise—a self-pasting scrapbook, a spiral hatpin, and a calendar watch fob were some of his inventions[8]—the Hannibal sage had no peer when it came to talking plain sense about autographs.

Consider the episode in Genoa, birthplace of Christopher Columbus, while Twain and his coterie toured the famous sites. "Come wis me, genteelmen," Ferguson said. "I show you ze letter-writing by Christopher Colombo! . . . Write it wis his own hand!" Twain's group obediently tagged along, and when the Columbus document had been laid out for their perusal, they viewed it noncommitally. Ferguson, accustomed to the oohs and ahs of rapturous tourists, grew agitated at the troupe's silence. "Christopher Colombo!" he said. "Ze great Christopher Colombo!"

The infamous doctor, a member of Twain's entourage who was handling the document at the time, remained nonplussed. "Ah," he said, "did he write it himself or—or how?"

"He write it himself! Christopher Colombo! His own handwriting, write by himself," Ferguson replied.

To which the doctor deposited the document on the table and said, "Why I have seen boys in America only fourteen years old that could write better than that."

"But zis is ze great Christo—"

"I don't care who it is," the doctor replied. "It's the worst writing I ever saw. . . . If you have got any specimens of penmanship of real merit, trot them out! And if you haven't, drive on!"[9]

ERRATA

Another huge item on the collectomaniac's agenda is mistakes— errors made in a book that send it soaring in value. And, curiously, the more glaring the mistake, the better. Say you pick off a shelf Sinclair Lewis's famed preacher novel, and you see on the binding the words "Elmer Cantry" instead of "Elmer Gantry."[10] What's your first thought? "Somebody in that publishing house screwed up royally. Right on the binding and everything. I hope that poor sap doesn't get sacked." Right?

And what's your second thought? "If they can screw up like that on the cover, who knows how many typos they let slip by inside. Darned if I'll buy this book." These are the thoughts of rational consumers.

But if you're a collectomaniac, you don't think like that. You think, "Unbelievable! A first-edition Lewis of imponderable value!" and you whip out your checkbook and write numbers with lots of zeros behind them.

I ask you honestly, does this make sense? Rewarding shoddy workmanship with honor? Tacitly encouraging mistakes? It does if you're not going to read the dad-blamed thing! And that's where the collectomaniac is coming from.

But enough about collectomania, for, when looked at through the wide-angle lens of all of biblioholism, collectomania remains in reasonable perspective. When compared to people who bury their books, or *eat* them, collecting them is tame. And it is to these other variants of biblioholism that we now turn.

CHAPTER SEVEN

Variants of the Disease

The bow too tensely strung

is easily broken.[1]

LET IT BE SAID THAT BIBLIOHOLISM is not an equal opportunity disease—some of us get the bug a lot worse than others. Like the biblioholics who protect their beloved tomes by interring them—either in some airless cabinet or in the ground—or the ones who derive a sadistic glee in destroying the things they love. And then there are the celebrated bibliophagi, whose idea of nutrition entails the introduction of pulp and ink to their digestive tracts. And who could overlook scholars, the ivory tower recluses who harbor a love unbounded for things inscrutable, and whose idea of a great read is a book with more footnotes than text? They line their studies with books, too, you know. Other biblioholics are even caught up in something so mundane as inveterate reading—that is, reading voluminously with little desire for acquisition.

All are biblioholics, and all deserve a spot on the continuum of addictive weirdness. But first, the more "normal" of these variant streams of the disease.

READAHOLICS

We see them in the office lunchroom, sequestered from the jabbering crowd, off at a table by themselves, eschewing sociability while their eyes fly through some thick tome. We see them on a bus bench, holding to their eyes a volume with a flashy cover, oblivious to the whirl of traffic at their feet. We even see them on city buses, with hands gripping an overhead strap, somehow able to keep their place in their book—and their feet on the floor—in spite of the apoplectic starting and stopping of the vehicle.

These are readaholics, a popular strain of biblioholism that makes its presence felt in all strata of society. They read anything at any time, anywhere. Most popular with readaholics is genre literature—romance, for example. Their books always seem to be of the same cut, with covers depicting a buxom lass, 85 percent décolletage, in some sort of passion-crazed dilemma, her raven hair fanning out in the winds of desire, with some sweaty stud behind her, his hands tenaciously gripping her shoulders and ready to move to more undulating terrain. Or they are quintessentially detective-like, with some sleuth looking suspiciously onto a blood-drenched corpse, with a fedora-topped villain showing us only his backside as he slips through a door.

Of course, we more "normal" biblioholics are forever reading, too. But what distinguishes us from readaholics is the simple fact that readaholics remember very little of what they read. All protagonists meld into one faintly defined figure; all plots coalesce into an amorphous series of actions and responses. But still, that's not enough, for many of us also fail to recall much of what we read. We need more clarification. So consider, then, these three chief characteristics of readaholism:

Variants of the Disease

* * *

1. The way readaholics describe the book in progress. They say things like "Oh, it's about this guy that goes around making all these women," and we don't know for sure if they're reading *Tom Jones* or Harold Robbins's *The Adventurers*. They never get too specific about anything they're reading.

2. The way they handle their books. Possession of those books is not a priority item. Some readaholics may have only a dozen books in their homes! Possession means nothing to the readaholic. Picking up a dozen books at the bookstore one day merely means they will have a dozen books to trade in the next time they visit—all of them read in the meantime, of course. For obvious reasons, the readaholic's most fertile hunting ground is the used bookstore.

3. They read *fast*. Now, be advised, not all fast readers are readaholics, but it is an indisputable fact that all readaholics can burn paper. This can be quite annoying for us slow-reading biblioholics. We see them at work one day just digging into a Michenerian purse-filler—they never read books of less than four hundred pages, it seems— and then a day and a half later we see them beginning a *different* Michenerian epic. And when we say, "Did you read all eleven hundred pages of *The Source* already?" they look at us like we just told them we had Elvis living in our guest room.

   Also, readaholics always seem to be boasting of their prolificness. They don't talk about the contents of the books they read; they talk about how long it takes them. They say things like, "Oh, I see you're reading Clancy's *Executive Orders*. I read that a couple of weeks ago during the commercials in *Friends*." Or "Hm-m-m, Don Delillo's *Underworld*, huh? That's a good book, but it'll take you two or three hours to read."

BIBLIOWEBBIES

This is the most recent breed of biblioholic to appear in our very circumscribed and parochial world. Because the Internet, in addition to doing everything else, also hawks books, it has become a prime location for the bookaholic to shop till he drops. After all, what could be easier, what could be more convenient, and until recently, what could be cheaper than zipping to Amazon.com and piling up volume after volume in one's cyber–shopping cart?

Alas, bibliowebbies are difficult to identify. Only those who succumb to this variation of the disease know who they are, for their book lives by necessity do not involve bookstores. They point and click and pick up packages at their door. That's the sum of the bibliowebbie book-buying and browsing experience. Book converse amid the civilizing aisles of a brick-and-mortar bookstore is replaced with chat-room dialogue where colloquists wear their emotions on their screens, lest any of their fellow confabulators be unable to parse out precisely the tone beneath their words. I am speaking, of course, of those ever-endearing emoticons here [☺].

It is also likely that bibliowebbies constitute the brunt of the e-book market as well. One not wholly conversant with the download culture is unlikely to buy one of these electronic products, for the simple reason that e-books do not actually exist in any spatial and concrete way. They constitute reading matter, true, but they are simply not real—there is no *there* there. They consist of colliding electrons traveling through wires into a screen. When you turn off the device upon which you are reading them, the e-book does not remain to be placed under your arm or on your shelf. It immediately teletransports into some cyber-library in some cyber-universe somewhere.

SCHOLARS

First, the qualification. Scholars, it is safe to say, get a bum rap in our society. A deluge of misinformation has successfully transformed those of scholarly persuasion—regardless of their physical features—into what is tantamount to a stereotype. But that stereotype—the scholar as a hunch-shouldered academician, eyes dimmed from reading with insufficient light, with glasses so thick that looking directly at the sun would burn a hole clean through his or her head; that image of an ivory tower recluse, burrowing deeper and deeper into the recondite recesses of some abstruse discipline, eschewing fashion and still clad in the same suits he had in his college years with lapels as wide as Baja California and fat little bib ties that stop just south of his titties, or still piling her hair up in one of those turn-of-the-century bread-loaf buns on the back of her head, unwilling to adapt to modern technological conveniences like plug-in irons and self-serve gas pumps (in short, the quintessential, all-American dweeb)—is greatly overstated. It doesn't fit the scholar of today, some of whom wear contacts, and sometimes even a bow tie.

But scholars of today, like their forebears in academe, still have books. Thousands of them, all lining floor-to-ceiling shelves, with piles knee-high in maze-like disarray covering vast portions of their den carpets.

Now granted, there's a lot of good we can say about scholars. They generally reflect on life's great issues. They seek the assumptions that lie beneath a given issue, and they bring to their quest epistemological and hermeneutical concerns. In short, they increase the realm of knowledge immeasurably.

But we come not to praise scholars—we come to rip them. For they are different from the average Joe and Jane Biblio. They live in a different world, speak a different lingo, and are invulnerable to the raging desires that tempt us ordinary book fiends for the following reasons:

* * *

1. Scholars get their books free. Publishers send them freebies; other scholars bestow on them gifts of books; some even receive a book allowance of hundreds of dollars from their schools. This allows them to sidestep some of the normal hardships of biblioholism. They eat meals, seek the conversation and congeniality of their peers, attend symposia, and take long trips in pursuit of their research. They hold the potential to live quasinormal lives, their every penny not being pumped into the acquisition of books.

2. They write books with titles like *Explorations in Accelerated Contextual Dimensions* and *Banana Slugs in Ecstasy: The Post-Precipitational Dance of Manumission in a*

Post-Darwinian Dialectic. Needless to say, nobody actually reads these books. (Scholars write them simply to keep from getting canned.) And they lace these tomes with heavily inspissated prose, turgid as *Ghostbuster* slime and plated with an armor of impenetrability capable of withstanding a wave of ICBMs. But of course, this is what the scholar wants. The world's leading scholar on subatomic particles in the Venusian atmosphere doesn't really want the world to understand what he or she is doing. To be known as the world's leading authority on subatomic particles in the Venusian atmosphere is enough.

3. Not only do they write books nobody else wants to read, they also *read* books nobody else wants to read. Their reading habits are *very* focused. This transmits to them the feeling of satisfaction derived from being part of an extremely closed circle of fellow travelers. They read some obscure book, clasp their hands behind their heads, lean back in their swivel chairs, and muse, "Just think, I may be only one of a half dozen people in the entire world who has read *An Ontological History of Nose-Boogers.*" When they pick up a copy of *U.S. News and World Report,* it's a walk on the wild side. And, despite their specialized interest, they're forever moaning and groaning about not being able to keep up with the literature in their field.

4. Their armpits get sweaty and their systolic heart rates hit three figures when they see a book heavy with footnotes. In fact, a great read for a scholar is a book whose endnote section is larger than the text itself.

5. Generally speaking, scholars are very spacey types. Oh, some are reasonably with-it, but most really don't have their fingers on the pulse of society. (They're too busy trying to find their own pulses.) They may know the latest theorum in the microbiological structure of this or that, but they didn't learn about the Vietnam War until campus radicals took over their offices and shut down the school.

* * *

BIBLIOTAPHS

It is a fine line we walk between sanity and madness in our book-love. Taking pride in a neatly stacked shelf is one thing, and wholly within the range of normalcy. Rising up in outraged disgust as some philistine commits crimes against our books—fingering them with dirty hands, setting sweaty beer cans on them, picking them off the shelf and within seconds defiling the spine with a crease—is the time-honored reaction of even the nonbiblioholic. All do it; all are suitably sensitized.

But as with all fine lines, this one becomes pretty broad when we consider the biblioholic excess of bibliotaphy—the burying of books. Although bibliotaphy encompasses also those biblioholics intent upon ensuring their books' safekeeping by lodging them away in safes and steel-lined rooms, these are not the extreme examples of the condition. The hard-core cases put them right into the ground.

Some do so out of messianic dreams. John Stewart, for example, believed humanity had a chance to make it in the long run only if his books—*The Apocalypse of Nature*, the *Harp of Apollo*, the *Sophiometer*—were saved from the conspiracies of world rulers of his day. He told his readers to bury their copies of his books "properly secured from damp, etc., at a depth of seven or eight feet below the surface of the earth," and then to divulge, only on their deathbeds, the world-saving tomes' whereabouts—and then only to the most trusting of confidants. Eventually, he believed, perhaps some generations into the future, mankind would have acquired the intellectual moxie to absorb his program.[2]

Others have taken their all-consuming love of books to more logical—if also more extreme—ends. After all, what greater act of love could biblioholics engage in than to pay the ultimate homage to their tomes by being buried *with* them? Eugene Field, who led a life of book-love, wrote of the dread that would descend upon him at the time of his final separation from his beloved volumes. He drew up a list of twenty-four books to be placed in his grave with the hopeful anticipation of more bookish days on the other side.

> *Then when the crack*
> *Of doom rolls back*
> *The marble and the earth that hide me,*
> *I'll smuggle home*
> *Each precious tome*
> *Without a fear a wife shall chide me.*[3]

More serious even than Field was the Wild West book-lover who had a precious volume inserted under his ribs and then was buried in a coffin made of his library bookshelves.[4]

These book buriers hold at least a pretense to sanity. Not so an English clergyman of the previous century, Mr. Anthony Horneck, who, having secured for a sovereign a prized rare copy of a sixteenth-century folio, perceived that the volume was "infected with worms—alive with them." Filled with apprehension that the insects would defile his entire library, he took prompt and effectual action to halt their advance: "I buried him underground, sir. Perhaps you don't know that garden mould is a remarkable purifier."[5]

BIBLIOCLASTS

Think back, fellow sufferers, to those carefree college days, when, amid all-night caffeine benders and midnight cram sessions, you let those opprobrious term papers slide until the very last day. And then when you finally got it together enough to truck down to the library, what did you find but that the very information you deemed absolutely essential to your thesis was housed in some reference books that, by library policy, were to remain on the premises at all times. And when you found it, it was five minutes before library closing, and the damnable paper was due first period in the morning. You've been there, I know. We all have. And unless you hail from highly puritanical stock, you allowed your gaze to furtively take in the room; you ascertained that no suspicious eyes observed your actions; and with one quick, violent sweep you ripped that page out of the book and stuffed it into your coat pocket.

If you did this or anything like it, you are a biblioclast. You are a destroyer of books. You may have repented of it since, but your action has placed you into the company of some very ignominious people.

Biblioclasts have never been at a want for reasons to destroy books. Some collectomaniacs of times past have destroyed others' books to make their own copies rarer. Others were moved by a demented perfectionism—they gathered up a number of imperfect copies of a book and, removing the flawed pages, substituted them with good pages and rebound them into an unmarred whole. Others still stripped a book clean of all illustrations or embellished capital letters. Censorious types ripped out offending pages. Those with a more salubrious motive retained only the best parts of a given book and bound them together. Our third president, for example, put together his own version of the Bible, composed of only the passages he liked. And others still went in for a more malicious sort of biblioclasm. One writer kept copies of books he disliked on his reading table and used pages from them to torch up his pipe.[6]

Even some very eminent personages have slipped into a book-destroying mode. Shelley sailed flyleaves as paper boats.[7] And scientist Charles Darwin cut heavy books in half to better work with them,[8] a practice the founder of neurology, Hughlings Jackson, also employed. When traveling by rail, Jackson often bought a novel to read on the trip and, once purchased, immediately ripped off the covers, tore the book in two and put half in one pocket and half in the other. A book clerk had the temerity to throw him a puzzled look once, and Jackson took the boy to task. "You think I am mad, my boy," he said to the clerk, "but it's the people who don't do this who are really mad."[9]

This sort of zaniness may seem pretty far out, well beyond the actions of the contemporary biblioholic. But, before we congratulate ourselves in our relative sanity, we should bear in mind that it is only a matter of degree. When we can, without a flush of guilt, tear that strip off an endpaper to serve as an emergency bookmark; when we, without even thinking about it, can do malicious damage to our books by turning down the pages; when we can fire a book at a cat in a fit of rage or prop up a sofa with a stack of volumes—can we really be that far from slipping into the deep water of biblioclasm?

BIBLIOPHAGI

Books—you sensuous things, you. You fill us with longing. To touch you, to allow us the tactile pleasure of stroking your smooth covers, to clasp you to our bosoms and emit perfervid groans of delight. To see you, aligned in uniform majesty on our shelves, your bindings ever so glossy, your cover illustrations and dust jacket megaportraits ever so inviting. To smell you, your ink and paper odors so intoxicating, so liberating to our pedestrian noses. (One contemporary biblioholic exults so in his olfactory powers that he claims to be able to discern publishing houses blindfolded simply by sticking his nose into the bindings of a book. Books from Mentor, he says, are primo sniffing.)

And—do not be taken aback by this concept—to eat you. Oh, we speak not of metaphorical consumption here—such as "devouring" the latest Clive Cussler, "nibbling at" the Garrison Keillor canon, "gourmandizing" Paul Johnson's histories. No, we're talking about the real thing.

Eating books. How better to become one with a beloved tome? How better to bring the words and thoughts of a revered writer directly into our being, to bridge the author–reader chasm and achieve the ultimate unity we all so ardently desire, than to physically chow down on a given volume? We speak of the celebrated bibliophagi, the real consumers of books. Want to be assertive? Don't read *Winning Through Intimidation*. Pop it into the Cuisinart with *The Art of Selfishness* and *eat it*. Want to talk like Shakespeare? Hunker down to *Othello* and *Hamlet* stew and allow the bard's diction to get to your brain via your stomach.

Sound crazy? Tell the Scandinavian political writer who was offered the choice of being beheaded or stepping up to a sumptuous repast of his own manuscript boiled in broth just how crazy he was.

Variants of the Disease

Tell it to satirist Isaac Volmer, who had to force down his literary efforts uncooked. Tell it to Philip Oldenburger, who was served up a dish of his own writing, which he had to eat while being flogged (the beating terminating only when the last morsel had been ingested).[10] Or to Theodore Reinking, a seventeenth-century polemicist, who was offered freedom from prison only if he ate a controversial book he had written, which he made more palatable with a special sauce.[11]

But bibliophagism is just *too* weird. It doesn't occur much among the contemporary book crowd. Far less eldritch, but far more prevalent, is a variant of the disease that strikes much closer to home for all of us—the dread and aggravating biblionarcissism. Who among us has not yearned to appear more bookish than we actually are? Who has not yielded to the temptation of affectation when talking books with our peers? We all have, and to some extent, we are all poseurs. In the next chapter we will learn how to transform this malady into a useful tool.

CHAPTER EIGHT

Biblionarcissism

Still am I busy bookes assembling,

For to have plentie it is a pleasaunt thing

In my conceyt, and to have them ay at hand,

But what they meane do I not understande.[1]

YOU SAY YOU'RE FEELING A LITTLE INSECURE about your bookish-ness these days? You're like everybody else in this tilt-a-wheel world, trying to structure a fulfilling existence around the bare minimums of time and energy, and you have far too many intrusions in your life to sit down night after night ingesting the contents of books. And when thrown into the company of other bookish sorts, you feel like a boom box in a string quartet. You don't know Goethe from Ginsberg, Updike from the Upanishads, and the Collinses—Jackie, Joan, and Wilkie—are one and the same to you. The yuppies in your social circle strike up a dialogue on the anomie that infests contemporary fiction, and you think Amy Tan is a celebrity chef on Food Network. You can't blow off an after-noon prowling the aisles of a bookstore and making yourself *au courant* on the titles. You can't even read all the catalogs you get in the mail. And yet you so desperately seek the status such book knowledge would bring.

Biblionarcissism

In times like these, when knowledge fails, you may find yourself resorting to one of the smarmiest ploys of all of biblioholism: posing. You may decide to play the biblionarcissist.

Biblionarcissism is one of the most virulent strains of biblioholism. And yet we may all fall prey to this odious tactic at one time or another. There is that oily undercurrent running through our minds that makes us want to appear as something we are not. Self-inflation, hypocrisy, egotism—unfortunate though they be—mark human nature.

But be advised, if you feel inclined to scrape the gutter in such a way, that biblionarcissism is tantamount to an art form. Convincing others that you are more bookish than you really are takes skill. First and foremost—and we hope we are not being too elementary here— you will need books. The household library. If bookish visitors are going to jump to snap conclusions about your pedigree from the titles in your library—and they are (we all do)—then you must take great pains to present an intelligent front. We will discuss the nature of these household volumes momentarily, but first, some tips on the actual presentation of these tomes:

* * *

1. Although hardbound books connote instant presence, an exclusive collection of the same is forced. It's *too* highbrow. Stick in a paperback here and there for verisimilitude.

2. Make sure the hardbound books you do purchase are properly broken in before putting them on the shelf. Also—and this may rankle the purists among us—beat on them a little before condemning them to years of mere pretentious show. Because, let's face it, you're not going

to be handling them much. Once they go onto the shelves, they may remain untouched until your next move. If one thing will unmask you as a charlatan, it is visitors pulling down a book from your shelf and having the bindings crack like a football player's knees when they open it.

3. For obvious reasons, make sure all the books are not of one color that matches the walls and curtains of your home. You want visitors to think you read more than *Architectural Digest*.

4. Don't intersperse them on your shelves with your knick-knacks. True biblioholics don't allow their books to share space with the ebony elephants and snow globes of their travels. And by all means, don't stick them in little openings next to your PC, with potted plants on every other shelf to present an esthetically pleasing visage. True biblioholics don't do that sort of thing. Books are to dominate the living area.

5. Although the temptation may be great, do not succumb to constructing shelves of dummy books. It has happened in the past. Book poseurs would set aside their top few shelves and build books out of wood, painting them decorous colors and embossing classical titles on the bogus wooden bindings. In ancient times this had been the particular proclivity of lawyers and physicians attempting to lend an air of prosperity to their chambers.[2] But clients and patients are in and out, so to speak, with hardly enough time even to write their checks. Visitors to your house may decide to check the

books out personally, and then you, the biblionarcissist, are had.

* * *

Which brings us to the contents of your show library. It has been said that one's library is a window unto one's soul. One can truly discern the contours of a person's interests, the inclinations of the mind, the power of the intellect, by perusing the titles on his or her shelves. Seeing a copy of the major works of every philosopher from Plato to Santayana in someone's bookcase gives you an idea of what that person is all about. It tells you something. Conversely, seeing bound volumes of the last twenty years of *MAD* magazine next to complete sets of the Garfield and Dennis the Menace oeuvres tells you something else.

Thus it will not wash to merely haul out all the books you've accumulated since sixth grade and range them in glorious array on your shelves. Many fall into this trap, setting dog-eared ninety-five-cent copies of *Oliver Twist* and *Wuthering Heights*—with "Reader's Supplement"—that they read as high school sophomores alongside a stuffy-looking *Introduction to Psychology*, with innumerable self-help books and gothic romances, some Sidney Sheldons, some Ken Folletts, a few travel books, coil-bindered instructional guides to their PC, and everything else they've ever read standing up in spartan regimen in a wall of shelves with big gaps everywhere—and they call it a library! No, it won't cut it. Even nonbiblioholics can see through that sorry dissimulation.

Buying the Harvard Classics en masse, Merle Johnson's "high spots," the Grolier Hundred, or all the books mentioned in Clifton Fadiman's *Lifetime Reading Plan* is effective, but there are dangers. Besides sucking your wallet dry overnight, you open your purported intellectual stature to inquiry. Your guests may solicit your view on, say, the nexus of thought between Hobbes and Marx, when the only nexus of thought you're aware of is the one between Hobbes and Calvin (not the reformer).

Much better is to request lists of books from an eclectic group of your acquaintances. Pick a classicist, a genre fan, a nonfiction aficionado, a biography nut—all different sorts—and ask them to draw up lists of great books for your personal consumption. This will endear you forever in these people's hearts—nothing so gratifies a biblioholic like being asked for a list of books to read. Plus it will give you an across-the-board array of titles from which to choose.

Which brings us to perhaps the most vital of all posing devices—bookmarks. What are you reading? How much are you reading? These are the questions at the forefront of all biblioholics' minds. Indeed, your bookmarks tell as much about you as do your books.

The simplest way to expose a nonbookish sort is to look at a wall of books and see absolutely no bookmarks in any of them. Either the owner plows through books from beginning to end with no cessation in reading whatsoever—never an aborted read, never a book that has bored him or her into narcoleptic halt. Or he or she doesn't read at all. With so few of the former in existence, it is best not to take chances. You need bookmarks as much as you need books. And not only one, but many. Approximately 10 percent of the books on your shelves should have bookmarks in them. Any more and you look like a dilettante, an unserious person. Any less and you look like a rube. Without seeming too elementary, it should be said that the books thus marked should be serious books. No bookmarks in *The Booger Book*, for example.

These should be changed regularly as well. In fact, one serious about presenting a bookish facade should set a time every week for the "changing of the marks," and do them all at the same time. Some books, of course, do not have to be changed quite so often. A bookmark stuck in the same page of Will and Ariel Durant's eleven-volume *The Story of Civilization* for the past fifteen years does not necessarily cast the poseur as a lightweight. But a stationary bookmark in *Who Moved My Cheese?* does. Also, no bookmarks in dictionaries, thesauruses, or other reference books, for obvious reasons.

TALK THAT TALK

Some read to think, these are rare;
some to write, these are common;
and some read to talk, and these form the great majority.[3]

By now you have come to learn that the mere presence of books does not a biblionarcissist make. Books are integral to the pose, to be sure. But there is more—infinitely more. You must be able to talk about them with a reasonable similitude to intelligence.

Again, we begin with the rudiments. Note this truth: Any book title or author name you intend to drop casually into a conversation must be pronounced correctly. We know it sounds almost too elementary to mention, but we cannot overstate this point. Hurling out a reference like "I found *L'Etranger* by Albert Camus to be seminal to my intellectual development" to a group of fellow bookaholics, but then letting the title come out like a native Texan ordering lunch in a Parisian cafe and, if that's not enough, capping the affair off by pronouncing the *s* on Camus, will send you packing quicker than a hometown fan after a visiting team's sudden-death field goal.

Take extreme care before dipping into foreign titles. Sure, it's a great coup if you pull it off, but if you don't, it will take a Berlitz course and a thousand profound but abstruse comments on the state of literature to win back your honor. So, play it very safe. Do you pronounce the final *e* in Hesse or not? Where is the emphasis on *My Antonia*? Are you really sure of how *The Brothers Karamazov* is pronounced? Does the cultured reader pause somewhere in "D'Urbervilles"? Is *Père Goriot* pronounced "Pear Go Riot"? *Jane Eyre* as "Jane Erie" (like the lake)? *Caveat poseur:* Know it or blow it.

This much is easy. Once engaged in actual conversation, however, the terrain gets infinitely more treacherous. You must have at your immediate behest a general recall of classics as well as current titles. Biblioholics, as a rule, are very literate. No name is too obscure, no topic too abstruse. Studying bestseller lists; picking phrases off dust jackets; scouring reviews; lifting a name or two from an index and trotting it out; spicing your dialogue with a French or German *bon mot* (properly pronounced, of course); memorizing *Bartlett's*—nothing can compare with these tactics to give you a ballpark talking knowledge.

But the dangers here are immeasurable. In his *Love Affairs of a Bibliomaniac*, Eugene Field tells of one such poseur who met his better while traveling England in an earlier century. While sharing a coach with a Greek scholar, this coxcomb "sought to air his pretended learning by quotations from the ancients."

The scholar called his bluff: "Pri'thee, sir, whence comes that quotation?" he asked.

"From Sophocles," the poseur replied.

To which the scholar said, "Be so kind as to find it for me?" And he pulled from his pocket a copy of Sophocles. The poseur, skilled at his craft, parried the thrust. It was not Sophocles, he said; he had meant

Euripides. To which the scholar produced, from his pocket, a copy of Euripides as well.[4]

Quoting authors or books while in near proximity to the volumes in question is tempting fate. Your comment may be challenged. And then, even as seen through Yogi's eyes, it's over.

The only fail-safe method of biblionarcissistic book talk is to be impenetrable. Obfuscation is power! Even a discussion of the latest diet book can be brought to a screeching halt with an obnubilated phrase or two. And really now, isn't that what you want? Heaven knows you don't want to actually talk about the book. Simply toss out a phrase, watch the heads tilt in query, watch the lips purse and the eyebrows soar, and stroll from the group in triumph. It sure beats arguing.

But what to say? That's the big question. To make things easier on the would-be biblionarcissist, we offer the following "Impenetrability Phrase Finder." Many such devices, highlighting bureaucratic jargon, have been invented specifically for various disciplines. These would

	1	2	3
1	literary-critical	construal	verisimilitude
2	ontological	epiphanical	textuality
3	sentimentalized	antitextual	hooey
4	mechanistic	minimalistic	eisegesis
5	synechdochal	deconstructive	syllabarium
6	holographic	syntactical	mimesis
7	bourgeois	impressionistic	totalities
8	structuralistic	neoclassical	twaddle
9	phenomenological	metalinguistic	metanarrative

probably suffice in a pinch, as the phrases concocted therein are equally inane, but the "Impenetrability Phrase Finder" goes directly to the heart of the bookish attitude. To use it, pick any three-digit number, say 793, and pick the appropriate word from each column, the 7 from the first column, the 9 from the second, and the 3 from the third. Put them together and you have your impenetrable phrase, in this case, "bourgeois metalinguistic hooey."

Once the time bomb of serious book discussion has been defused, you can enter another fertile field for biblionarcissists: talking about writers' lives, information for which can be derived from reviews and the ubiquitous writer interviews that inexorably follow a writer's first big success. Why, even selective perusal of *Good Morning America* or *People* magazine can provide enough information to at least avoid embarrassment.

Everybody knows about Tom's white suits, about Norman's little knife fight with his wife, that Saul went through a big-money divorce, that Denmark didn't work out for Garrison. As essayist Joseph Epstein said, "We have among us today so many would-be Boswells, and no Dr. Johnsons whatsoever."[5]

This may be bad for literature in general, but for biblionarcissists it is the stuff of *Te Deums*. It means they will not be elbowed out of cocktail party palaver simply because they haven't read the books being discussed.

And that brings up another vital plate to your biblionarcissistic armor. To pose with power, inscribe this dictum on your memory: At no time, and under no circumstance, allow yourself to admit that you have not read a book. Admit such to your fellow conversationalists and you'll be exiled to the bean dip, talking about the merits of the spreadsheet format of Windows 98, the number of reps you pull on the health club lat machine, and the St. Louis Rams' offensive scheme. You have *always* read the book in question.

Granted, to imply such may reveal some worn spots in your cloak of dissimulation, for, indubitably, you have *not* read every book being discussed. However, writer Tad Tuleja has come to your rescue with his ground-breaking tome, *The Catalog of Lost Books*. While Tuleja wrote his book as an antidote to the pedantic and unabashedly self-serving palaver one encounters while hobnobbing at your basic hoity-toity cocktail confab, it can serve the budding biblionarcissist as well. Tuleja once overheard a highbrow intone, "Ontologically speaking, Pantagruel is bodied forth with less amplitude of vision than any other character in the picaresque tradition." To which another egghead replied, "*Bien sur*, but in terms of sheer facticity, don't you agree that the Rabelaisian oeuvre is still the acme of the genre?"

Tuleja is most certainly no book poseur, but his response to the aforementioned discussion is one all nascent poseurs should go to school on, to wit: "If you chaps want the acme of the picaresque," he said, "surely you're tilling the wrong field. The genre didn't peak until 1845. Myra Quinn's *Six Years with a Donkey*. Magisterial."[6]

It stopped the highbrows' tongues faster than a denied application for tenure. How can anyone reply intelligently to the citation of an author and a book that the speaker has *made up on the spot?* Anything less than complete corroboration of your statement puts them in danger of being shown up. And if they do respond, you simply carry on with more details of your bogus book.

Coupling a store of precogitated bogus book titles along with a ready and arcane vocabulary of elitist phrases—the "Impenetrability Phrase Finder" can help you there—can thrust a cob into the mouth of any elitist worth his or her "-ization" word endings. But it requires a peripatetic imagination and a ready repository of bogus books and authors. In short, it's a heckuva lot of work. Much better—and much easier—is to rely on these prescripted responses:

* * *

"I skimmed it" or "I browsed it" (thus I have assimilated the big picture and can talk of it on a cosmic scale, but don't expect me to regurgitate the details).

"I'm at it now" (that is, I always have major books in progress and can only refer to it in an inchoate way).

"I read it when I was young" (thus absolving me from any expectation to quote it, recall minor characters, recall major characters, discourse on plot or literary conventions, or speak of it in any other than the most rudimentary terms).

* * *

WALK THAT WALK

There is, however, another venue that is equally ripe for the poseur: the bookstore itself. Where else is one guaranteed a population of so many people with bookish predilections gathered all in one place, all picking books off the shelves and flipping through pages with studied and discriminating eyes? Where else is the general conversation at such a heightened level? Many plums can be plucked from this ripened tree, many reputations made in these lettered aisles. And besides, these people are all *strangers*. Their judgment of you will be based on what they see that one time. They don't know if you have two books at home or twenty thousand.

Plus, the bookstore environment lends itself exceedingly well to the pose. The protocols—although unwritten—are nearly identical to those in place at a library, and that means even the most outrageous comment on your part will be met with impunity. Is somebody you've never seen before going to call you down in the sepulchral quiet of a bookstore as you discourse on "ontological antitextual totalities"? (That's 237 on your "Impenetrability Phrase Finder.") Trust me, it won't happen.

But there's more than talk involved. There is *bookstore presence.* With what gait will you stroll among the shelves? What discriminatory eye will you cast on the volumes? What degree of asperity will spread across your face as you reject a volume from an inferior writer? Every bookstore move sends a message; the pose is paramount.

We go to the ancients for direction. Bookstore posing is a time-honored tradition, employed by the poseur from the time bookstores were invented. The following anecdote, written in 1606, touches many posing high points:

> This great linguist my Maister, will march through Paules Church-yard. Come to a booke binders shop, and with a big Italian looke and spanish face aske for these bookes in spanish and Italian, then turning through his ignorance, the wrong ende of the booke upward use action, on this unknowne tongue after this sort, first looke on the title and wrinckle his brow, next make as though he read the first page and bites a lip, then with his naile score the margent as though there were some notable conceit, and lastly when he thinkes hee hath gulld the standers by sufficiently, throwes the booke away in a rage, swearing that he could never finde

bookes of a true printe since he was last in Joadna, enquire after the next marte, and so departs.[7]

It's all there: the pretentious demeanor carried on despite profound ignorance, the facial contortions of disdain, the supercilious examination of the book's lineaments, the conscious attempt to attract a gaggle of sycophantic onlookers, and the contemptuous casting aside of the examined volume. Except for the bit about looking at the book upside down, it is a portrait of bookstore posing.

In many respects, our ancestors in affectation had it much easier than we do when it comes to this refined science. After all, there was far more to examine. Those folks could sashay into a bookseller's shop and consume hours examining one book: the margins, the binding, the paper, the type, the engraving, title pages, gilt edges, watermarks, the provenance of the books, and a score of other esoteric considerations. Some of them whipped out a device called an Elzevirometer and actually measured the margins on the spot. And that's all before they had to read a single word.

Today's biblionarcissist has no such advantage. What's there to examine? The author's portrait on the dust jacket? The quality of the glue that binds the paperback? Would anyone really ever decide against a book because the typeface is incongruous with the message? Today's poseur must be intellectual in his or her posturing.

The poseur's first order of business upon entering a store is to gather up an armful of heavy-duty tomes—books which, by their very titles, will accrue intellectual weight. Depending, of course, on what is available, these volumes should speak for themselves—and for you:

* * *

A volume or two by authors who have only one name (Madonna, Cher—oops—I mean Thucydides, Epictetus, Juvenal, etc.).

Books with impressive titles that give onlookers the feeling that if they don't recognize the title, they at least should (*Leviathan, Critique of Pure Reason, The Varieties of Religious Experience, An Enquiry Concerning Human Understanding,* etc.).

A book or two that mark you as your own thinker, cut apart from the herd (something by a little-known Bulgarian novelist, or the musings of some obscure Portuguese poet— in Portuguese).

A couple of books that most people have heard of, but don't have the guts to tackle (Proust's *Remembrance of Things Past,* John Calvin's *Institutes of the Christian Religion,* Pynchon's *Gravity's Rainbow,* etc.).

A few Viking Contemporaries or other design paperbacks to announce one's place on the cutting edge of fiction.

* * *

Nota bene: We're not advocating buying these books, but merely suggesting that you stick a few of them under your arm and parade around the bookstore. This establishes the tone of your visit and will deflect any suspicious eye that might alight on you once you start walking that bookish walk and talking that bookish talk.

But perhaps the most powerful pose of all is that of imitating an author. This scores big-time points in all onlookers' eyes and can be most effectively played out by strolling into the store with certain questions already in mind and then accosting bookstore clerks with a barely suppressed rage that is loud enough for everyone within thirty feet to hear. Joseph Epstein lays out an effective line of six authorial questions in his book of essays *Once More Around the Block*, four of which are recapped here:

* * *

1. "Why isn't my book displayed prominently in the window? . . ."
2. "Why isn't my book on the bestseller table? . . ." [I might add, do *not* ask, "Why is my book on the 80-percent-off table?" because the biblionarcissist would not choose to "author" such a clunker in the first place.]
3. "Why is it shelved under Sociology or under Self-Help? . . ." [When in reality it is a quasiphilosophical guide to the meaning of life, a Rorschach test made plain.]
4. "Why . . . isn't it even in the store? . . ."[8]

* * *

Then, after a brief interrogation of bookstore personnel, take your pose to the hoi polloi—the common bookstore browser. Best is to walk directly to an aisle where one of your "books" could plausibly be shelved. (This is somewhat tricky. For example, stay away from the Classics section. Never say, "*Finally,* they're stocking my book," while pointing to a book like *Madame Bovary*. Or, if handling the book in question is desired, make sure no megaportrait of the real writer is spread across the back of the dust jacket.)

Next, let loose with veiled but self-adulatory comments directed toward anyone who happens to be standing nearby. The following will give you an idea:

*   *   *

"You know, strangely, I don't mind being called a minor writer."

"Those editors at *The New Yorker* accepted my piece three weeks ago and they're still sitting on it."
"Cliffs Notes said the contract was in the mail, and as soon as I get it, I'll start on my next novel."

"Can you believe that a sociological work of such puissance as my *Hard Hats and Soft Noggins* would fail to take off in this country?"

"Sure, *Lake Wobegon Days* was a monster, but what I want to know is does Keillor know the *craft*?"

"Moyers only agreed to give me a half hour. I laughed in his face."

"Then those rubes at Random House changed a semicolon to an em-dash and I told them to stick it. 'Send the manuscript back,' I said. Oh, they begged unconscionably. But hey, I don't have to put up with that stuff."

*   *   *

At any rate, you get the idea. And don't be worried about laying it on too thick. This is impossible. As Joseph Epstein has remarked, when it comes to praise, authors don't know the meaning of the word *fulsome*.[9]

However, we have run somewhat far from the field of genuine biblioholism in this chapter. Posing, while time-honored and very ecumenical in appeal, is still a stepchild of bona fide book-madness— it is an aberration. When it comes right down to it, we want to agree with Sir William Waller who said, "Books were made for use, and not for ostentation, . . . in vain do they boast of full libraries that are contented to live with empty heads."[10]

Empty-headed or not, we must move on. But since we *are* in a bookstore, let's get down to the nub of the disease: the actual buying of the books. You are what you buy, and in the next chapter we will set out to prove it.

CHAPTER NINE

We Are What We Buy

Alas! Where is human nature so weak as in the book-store!

Speak of the appetite for drink; or of a bon-vivant's relish

for a dinner! What are these mere animal throes

and ragings compared with

those fantasies of taste, of those yearnings

of the imagination, of those insatiable appetites

of intellect, which bewilder a student

in a great bookseller's temptation-hall?[1]

THE BOOKSTORE—SHANGRI-LA, CAMELOT, the Seven Cities of Cibola, Nepenthe, Oceana, and Erewhon all rolled into one. Utopia and dystopia—it's where the excesses of our biblioholism are on ready display. Oh, those happy aisles, those euphoric shelves—there's something about them that sends a biblioholic into delirious profligacy.

Certainly, it's nice to sit at home reading them; it's pleasant to carry them home on loan from the local library. But when it comes right down to it, that's not where we're at. To put that fire in our belly and that sparkle in our eyes, well, give us a bookstore any old time. Nothing touches the ecstasy of actually buying books, of getting our predaceous little hands on them for keeps. The bookstore—that's where the biblio-holism in all of us shines.

Take the English statesman William Gladstone, for example. Now, there was a man who knew how to buy books. He had no conscience whatsoever in sating his biblioholic desires. Bibliophile Eugene Field once had occasion to witness Gladstone's book-buying habits firsthand. Field had wandered into a bookshop to ply his craft one day when he heard the proprietor ask Gladstone, who was also shopping there, "What books shall I send?" To which the statesman swept his arm grandly about the premises and gave the peremptory reply, "Send me *those!*" after which he marched out the door. Field then stepped to the counter with a volume in hand and as he anted up for the book was told that it was already sold. "Sold?" Field cried. "Yes, sir," the propri-etor returned. "Mr. Gladstone just bought it; I haven't a book for sale—Mr. Gladstone just bought them *all!*" Gladstone had, with that one grandiose gesture, bought the entire store. In fact, according to the bookseller, buying entire stores was something of a regular practice for Gladstone. Indeed, it was the third time he had cleaned the man out.[2]

Few of us have the means—or the shelf space—to play the role of a modern-day Gladstone. And a good thing it is too, for this sort of buying strategy, although seemingly quite rewarding on the surface, can come back to haunt us—as it did to Gladstone. Every once in a while, the sheer volume of his library forced him to take inventory and cull out the less desirable of his massive purchases. He sold these to the propri-etors of used bookstores, who later sold them back to him—at advanced prices.[3] And why not? Suckers like that are *not* born every minute.

Gladstone, although bolder than most, was not unique in those early book days. Others were equally rapacious in their shopping habits. Quite a few noblemen of yore made it their practice to purchase entire libraries en bloc when a noted bibliophile went up to that big bookstore in the sky. After all, it made sense, if one had the money. No guesswork, no mingling with the hoi polloi, no sorting and deciding in the cramped and uncomfortable bookseller's shop. "Just bring them over," they commanded. "I'll keep what I want and toss the rest."

A man named Naude, buying by proxy for a Cardinal Mazarin, on one occasion left a town in his wake "as bare of printed paper as if a tornado had passed through, and blown the leaves away."[4] And English bookman Richard Heber once bought thirty thousand in a single sitting.[5]

But the book world was a trifle different in those days. The paperback revolution with its sweep of cheap editions had yet to engulf the planet. Average Joes and Janes were financially indisposed to enter the fray. Biblioholics, by and large, were men of means who scoured the land for the few copies available, obsessed in their passion and oblivious to the word *no*. These guys were *serious*. Nothing could thwart them from their purpose. Lord Spencer once consumed a year of his life in Rome in monomaniacal pursuit of a copy of the *Martial* of Sweynheym and Pannarz (1473), without visiting the Coliseum or the Vatican. When he found it, his departure was immediate; he couldn't be bothered with any tourist attractions on the return trip either.[6]

The book world was also intense in those days. Fights occasionally broke out in bookstore aisles. When the English translation of *The Devil on Two Sticks* came out, the books were gobbled up insatiably, to the point that, when two noblemen entered a shop where one copy of the book remained, the lords drew swords. Only the intervention of the bookseller with a borrowed copy of the *casus bellus* precluded the letting of blood.[7] When John Morley's *Life of Gladstone* came out in 1903, the chaotic scene in the Macmillan offices made the run on *Harry Potter and the Goblet of Fire* look like a couple of tykes arguing over who gets *The Cat in the Hat* at the neighborhood bookmobile.[8] Today, the only place one experiences this sort of intensity is at the martial arts exhibitions that are euphemistically called "Friends of the Library" sales.

But times have changed. Few of us have the resources to merely grab and run these days. There's the money problem, the space problem, the time problem, besides which there is always that guilt, the angst that forever gnaws at our souls. Indiscriminate buying is not really an option. We must be circumspect in our book-buying habits, pulling meat from the confection.

So our question becomes: How do we purchase in mass large enough to stay our book stomachs, and yet emerge some hours later still on the lee side of sanity? How do we rationalize away this attack on our wallets?

Whether we know it or not, each of us walks through the hallowed bookstore portals with a strategy. Some are transparent—to buy a particular book, to enrich ourselves in a given discipline or genre—but others are opaque. And, to be blunt, very strange. For example, why are we toting the entire corpus of an unknown Algerian diarist? Why is that stack of books under our arm a microcosm of the current bestseller list? Why are we plopping down good money for books on math when we have long ago acknowledged that we were "word persons"?

There's a reason. We are playing out a coherent, and oft-times subliminal, rationale for buying books. And it's insidious as well, for each of our strategies is open-ended. Biblioholics, as a rule, do not walk into a bookstore with the intention of buying *just one book*. Or, if by chance we do walk in with such a purpose, we never walk out that way. There is a higher power that guides our steps, that allows us to dowse the fires of guilt that rage within our souls.

What, then, are these unnamed forces? What weird and self-condemning rationalizations course through our brains as we stroll the aisles? In short, how do biblioholics buy books?

THE MONEY-LIMIT BUYER

Some of us buy books in much the same way as a heavy drinker attempts to control whiskey intake, scribing a mark with a diamond ring on a whiskey bottle two fingers down and saying, "Thus far and no farther." Only we do it with money. We walk through the bookstore door with a set amount in mind, and we purpose to spend no more. This rationale allows biblioholics to engage their mania under the pretense that they have at least some measure of control over themselves. It's simple and it makes sense, and it even works on occasion.

But it does create unique bookstore behavior. Money-Limit Buyers can be recognized by their constant shuffling of their stack of books, putting one back, picking another up, now with seven, then with four, trading two $9.95 paperbacks for a $19.95 hardback, and so on. They are always cognizant of the self-imposed limit. Unfortunately, in the latter stages of the disease, the limit has a way of growing. Biblioholics always need more books to satiate their hunger.

THE NO-MORE-THAN-$5.95 SHOPPER

A variation of the Money-Limit Buyers, No-More-Than-$5.95 Shoppers set a financial ceiling for each book they buy. By telling themselves they will buy no book priced over $5.95, they delude themselves into thinking they are in control. In most cases, however, the reverse is true.

A biblioholic can go just as crazy with cheap books. One such biblioholic emerged from a bookstore once with the entire P. G. Wodehouse corpus in tow—and the man wrote ninety-some books (not all of which, luckily for this biblioholic, were in print). But all were priced at $4.95.

THE YOU-CAN'T-GO-WRONG-FOR-SEVENTY-FIVE-CENTS RATIONALE

This is a mind-set common to all biblioholics. Say you have had a productive day in the aisles; a stack of purchases rests in your hands. And those are it; you intend to buy no more. Yet you are caught up in the contagious ambience of the place. You can't leave yet. So, with the ostensible motive of innocent browsing, you continue your rounds. And what do you see but a Barthelme marked down, all sorts of early le Carrés at 80 percent off, a complete set of Annie Dillard at a ridiculously low price. Sure, you've already shot your wad; you've satiated the voracious appetite. But for seventy-five cents you can't go wrong, and you plop a couple bargain books onto your stack.

And, of course, the amount is relative. One person's seventy-five cents may be another person's $4.95. If you're looking at a $120.00 bill for half a dozen hardbound new releases, what's another three $4.95 bargains, right? So what if you won't get at them right away? So what if you won't get at them at all? Your conscience is quelled because you got a bargain.

Some biblioholics limit their purchases to *only* bargain books. And in many ways, this rationale is entirely sane. They are moved by a motivation similar to that of buyers who refuse to buy hardbound books, reasoning that within a year's time that $22.95 tome will be available, still new, still pretty, in paper for half the cost. Only they take it a step further. Why not, they think, merely wait a few months more and pick it up for $2.00 or $3.00 on the bargain shelf or at a second-hand shop? It makes sense, commercewise. But biblioholism transcends commercial wisdom. The biblioholic appetite is not sated merely by the getting of a deal. If biblioholics can pick up fifteen books for $45.00 at a secondhand store, saving perhaps $60.00 off the cover price, why not, their insidious minds reason, spend the $60.00 they saved on twenty more books? The fact is, biblioholism is appeased by volume alone. This is why one occasionally sees rental trucks outside the doors of used bookstores.

ULYSSESIZATION

We are finite creatures. We live, and we will die. We only have so much time, so much intellectual energy, so much cognitive power, so many light bulbs. But there are oh so many books to read. And some of them are pretty dang tough to understand. What is Thomas Pynchon talking about in *Gravity's Rainbow*? Where is William Faulkner coming from when he pens large sections of his fiction without punctuation or capitalization? Who are these guys Daedalus and Bloom and what are they doing for six hundred pages? Does Virginia Woolf ever get *To the Lighthouse* or what?

We don't know, true. In fact, many of us might not even care. Personally, I would rather assemble a 1,500-piece puzzle of a Jackson Pollock painting than slog through *Finnegans Wake*. But this is a wholly unacceptable biblioholic attitude. We can't not care. True biblioholics never write off an author merely because that author is inscrutable. Inability to access the inaccessible is the exclusive province of the rank amateur. We *have* to care.

So what do we do? Take three months out of our lives and plow through these abstruse volumes? Given copious periods of time and an armory of Cliffs Notes, anybody can make nugatory and strictly superficial sense out of them. But we, being buying and reading biblioholics, don't have the former, and we wouldn't be caught dead in public with the latter. So we do the next best thing: we buy books about the difficult book and its author. Commentaries. Biographies. Ancillary and related works. We stack these up in splendid array, occasionally bringing them into our laps to breeze through the index, scan a paragraph, get acquainted with the table of contents, or read the first and last chapters. Those books feed our vanity. They make us feel smart, intellectual, and able to at least keep within the outskirts of coherence when the book comes up over white wine and brie.

MICHENERITIS

There they stand: foreboding, ominous, inches thick and taunting. "Go ahead," they say. "Pick me up. Get hooked on me. I will control your life for weeks, maybe months."

These are the big books. And while they frighten many biblioholics—after all, they are thick (*Sacajawea* is *two inches* thick), usually have a myriad of characters, and take ever so long to read—some book buyers are inexorably drawn to them, for they do provide a certain grotesque sort of gratification. Take readers of James Michener's *Centennial*, a 1,086-page recounting of the history of a Colorado town that begins its narrative a millisecond or two after the beginning of time. Readers wade through a tour of the inner earth complete with tectonic plates, then tread with dinosaurs, swim with prehistoric beavers, romp with horses and buffalo, and finally, on page 150 or so, the plot takes an extremely dramatic twist—a human being is introduced to the plot. Then there's the trip up the Missouri, the big cattle drive, the Mexican-American war, the railroad, the mutton-beef wars, and countless other events of frontier history to traverse until finally, many, many pages later, readers can finally snap closed the cover on this epic story and move on to other fare. Sure, they could have copped out and watched the miniseries, but no, they tackled the book, reading every last page. And now that they're done, they deserve something for their effort, right?

This is the mind-set common to Micheneritis sufferers. They're constantly bragging about the size of the books they read. Indeed, they can be recognized by the sneer of superiority that spreads across their faces whenever they discuss books. They know that when they hit page 300—a place in most novels where readers are normally going into the long slide to the plate—the big-book readers are still early in the count. It takes a special sort of person, they believe, to tackle these monsters of print. One with staying power, one with discernment, one who can keep two hundred characters apart, one with a Jerry Lucas memory.

Some, of course, search out shortcuts. A few biblioholics skip all the descriptive paragraphs in the books they read, concentrating solely on dialogue. It takes them twenty minutes to read a Balzac. But these are the exception rather than the rule.

CONTINGENCY BUYERS OR
THE GOING-WHERE-NO-MAN-HAS-GONE-BEFORE SYNDROME

This particular book buyer is forever asking the question, What's the next hot trend in the information business? What are people going to want to know about? What countries will emerge in future years as world trouble spots or idyllic and pristine tourist wonderlands? What rave and heretofore unheard-of sport or recreation will sprout up from obscurity? Who will be the new exploding star in the self-help heavens? Where do we go after collagen injections and liposuction and tanning salons and emotional intelligence and Montana and Prozac and Deepak Chopra and all this right brain–left brain stuff?

Good questions all. And Contingency Buyers want to know the answers. So they buy books with a predictive mentality; they anticipate where the world is going and they prepare themselves for the journey. In this way, no trend catches them unawares. When the topic is broached, they merely waltz to their library and pull the seminal works from their shelves, where they have been standing for the past five years.

THE NOTHING-HERE-BUT-US-LEMMINGS BUYER

Antipodal in attitude to the Contingency Buyer are the Nothing-Here-But-Us-Lemmings Buyers. These buyers take absolutely no chances in their purchases, employing a very cautious buying strategy that may stem from any number of causes. One of which might be that they can't think for themselves. From childhood on, someone has always been choosing their books for them. The little boys got Chip Hilton or Tom Swift or the Hardy Boys; the little girls were handed Nancy Drew and Cheryl Ames. And today, someone is still choosing their books for them—other consumers. They don't buy anything that is not on the bestseller lists.

Or, the buyers may have no taste or discretion in books whatsoever. A book is a book is a book, and whether it be at the conclusion of *Sweet Savage Surrender* or *Anna Karenina,* they snap the book shut and sigh the sigh of accomplishment regardless. Bestseller lists lead them out of this wilderness of indiscretion.

Or it might be totally cosmetic. The bestsellers do look nice in the stacks; they do emit a fragrance of contemporaneity. And the sensitive biblioholic socialite may be compelled to take his or her buying cues from proven sources.

Whatever the reason, look for only the time-worn and well-tested titles on these buyers' shelves. *Reader's Digest* condensed versions are big with these buyers; their bookstore visits are confined to the new releases rack; and their shelves look like they were stocked by a Book-of-the-Month Club sales rep.

THE DISCOVERY BUYER OR THE I-KNEW-GARP-BEFORE-ROBIN-WILLIAMS BUYER

It's cocktail hour with the biblioholics and the Johnny-come-lately host is trumpeting the satiric genius of Evelyn Waugh. He's claiming all sorts of simpatico with the English satirist, championing his vision, reveling in his subtle but stabbing wit. You know Waugh, too, and this guy's hubris is starting to bug you. So you traipse to his shelves for corroboration of his boasts, and yearning to debunk the man, you pull down a copy of *Handful of Dust* and—voilà!—the man is unmade. Rupert Graves, Kristin Scott Thomas, and James Wilby (the cast from the recent movie) are on the cover. And furthermore, his copy of *Brideshead Revisited* sports cover photos of Jeremy Irons, Laurence Olivier, and all sorts of other actors.

If these are the sorts of things you are sensitive to, you are probably a Discovery Buyer. Your *Handful* was printed before the movie, your *Brideshead* before the *Masterpiece Theatre* presentation.

125

It takes no prescience whatsoever to jump on a writer's success train once it's rolling to stardom. What does take prescience—and moxie and intelligence and discrimination—is to be on board while it's still in the station. And Discovery Buyers buy books with this in mind. Their *Nicholas Nickleby* doesn't have Roger Rees on the cover. They were ardent admirers of Russell Baker even before the *Time* magazine cover. They thought John Updike was great way back in the 1950s when he was a staffer at *The New Yorker.* They read *84 Charing Cross Road* before the movie. Heck, they even read *Bambi* before the movie. And their *Garp* is solid blue with gold lettering—and *without* Robin Williams.

But there are gradations to discovery buying. In fact, in our world of cross-cultural media saturation, there is a definite pecking order to fame. And it is the Discovery Buyer who wants to get in on the ground floor, or at least on the terrace level.

Ergo, the Discovery Index, the Discovery Buyer's guide to buying prescience.

* * *

The Discovery Index
You Knew the Author . . .

BEFORE the author's short stories appeared in a regional literary review.

AFTER short stories appeared but before novel appeared in hardback.

AFTER novel in hardback but before laudatory reviews.

We Are What We Buy

AFTER laudatory reviews but before novel comes out in paperback.

AFTER novel comes out in paper but before in-depth author interview in *Partisan Review* or other weighty periodical in which author speaks of this microcosm that is life.

AFTER in-depth interview but before novel appears on bestseller lists.

AFTER appearance on bestseller lists but before author's ominous rumblings on social issues in the local press.

AFTER social rumblings in local press but before *New York Times* profile.

AFTER *New York Times* profile but before novel is produced as miniseries or movie.

AFTER miniseries or movie but before paperback is reissued with TV or movie stars on cover.

AFTER paperback reissued with TV or movie stars on cover but before appearance of TV or movie stars on *Good Morning America*.

AFTER TV or movie stars appear on *GMA* but before novelist is on show.

AFTER novelist appears on *GMA* but before novelist is profiled in *People*.

AFTER *People* but before *Time* or *Newsweek* cover.

AFTER *Time* or *Newsweek* cover but before book is issued on tape.

AFTER book is issued on tape.

* * *

With this index in mind, Discovery Buyers prowl the bookstores, always seeking the unknown writer, always buying books that no one has ever heard of. And then when placed in social settings, they lord it over their less percipient peers.

However, the Discovery Index is no hard-and-fast guideline. There are exceptions to the Discovery Index, like the Garrison Keillor Syndrome. The Discovery Buyer would never be fooled by one claiming first rights as a Keillor aficionado who had come on board after *Lake Wobegon Days* and before the *Prairie Home Companion* on Public Radio. Or a Bill Buckley fan who said he joined the crowd after *Saving the Queen* but before *Firing Line* on PBS.

THE SELF-HELPIST

Of all the rationales for buying books, none is more straightforward than the Self-Helpist's. There is no deception, no duplicity, in this buyer's bookstore visit. No rationalizations or justifications. No mind games or subtle interplay of inner voices, hashing out the ethical propriety of every expenditure. We biblioholics are forever saying that we need books, we must have books to live, and so forth. When we make such comments we speak on an exclusively metaphorical plane—be real, we aren't really going to die if we don't have books. However, Self-Helpists operate under a far more utilitarian rubric. These are folks who need a how-to book to get out of bed in the morning. They probably *will die* if they don't have their self-help books.

Self-Helpists are always seeking help. Unfortunately, they seek that help where it can least be found—in the self-help section of the bookstore. Biblioholism is but a cross-addiction for Self-Helpists and should not be treated per se. They've got a lot bigger problem than buying too many books.

Getting Them into the House

Say we've been hanging one on at the local bookstore, picking books off the shelves in manic glee, luxuriating in the euphoria that is out-of-control buying. Our nagging conscience has been muted temporarily, our sense of responsibility stifled. We are simply too high to let anything bother us. A eudaemonic rush suffuses our entire being—this is what it's all about; it doesn't get any better than this. We get into our car and our spirits are soaring like pterodactyls in flight.

But then, about the time we hit that last stoplight before pulling into our driveway, we suffer a bout of reality therapy. The devious nature of the disease sets in, and the big question hits us: How are we going to get these books past our spouse? The cruel, unsympathetic, minatory helpmate, all suspicion and no compassion, towering ever in our minds, wielding a rolling pin or a Black &

Decker chain saw, as the case may be, threatening severe bodily impairment or incessant verbal obloquy if we so much as walk through the door with a new and desirable tome tucked under our arm. Yes, getting the books past that redoubtable monster is a challenge. How're we going to do it?

Obviously, concealment of the tomes is *de rigueur.* The loose-fitting clothes, the huge pockets, the layered look, the anchorman trench-coat with pockets everywhere—all are effective for concealing small quantities of small tomes. However, one must be wise. There's always the chance that the biblioholic, big bulky coat with pockets bulging everywhere, may look more like he's just returned from an assault on the North Face of Annapurna than a trip to the bookstore. Also, the Quasimodo look—stuffing the books in a backpack over which a coat is worn—has been used with some effect, although generally only by natural hunchbacks and leftover 1960s types.

But there are limits to how many books can be strapped onto the body, and this method is usually effective only with small tomes. Larger tomes must be concealed in something we are carrying into the house. A stack of lumber, for example. Although this may give rise to unwanted questions—for example, "Why are you carrying that lumber to your study?"—it is dependable at least once. Much better is the briefcase—not one of those sleek attaché jobs, but an enormous, bulky number currently used only by university profes-sors in their eighties. By putting the books in the trunk, biblioholics can embark upon frequent trips to the car under the artifice that they must work on it—check the oil, fix the windshield wipers, clean the turn signals, and the like—while dragging a briefcase on every trip, filled with booty on the way in, empty on the way out.

But these are very elementary ploys. The intelligent spouse will be onto them immediately. Hard-core biblioholics employ far more devious stratagems. To this end, consider the advice given by Ben Abramson in his essay "On Getting Books into the Home." Abramson advocates depositing the tomes at the office immediately after purchase. That night at home the biblioholic would remove an equal number of books from the shelf and stack them under the bed. The next day he or she would haul the new books in and put them in the vacated spot on the shelf. The ruse carries with it the presumption that the obvious place to look for new books would be under the bed, not in the stacks. The spouse sees the old books under the bed, curiosity is not raised, and the freshly purchased volumes are overlooked on the shelf. It sounds pretty good on paper. However, the method fails to resourcefully address the sticky problem of getting the books into the house, for here Abramson advocates concealing them *in one's pants*.[1]

Some of Abramson's other tactics are equally devious in nature. One consists of inveigling the bookseller to send the books to your house as a gift from a fictitious donor. Another entails placing a plain, unmarked parcel—containing the books, of course—on your doorstep and allowing your spouse to discover it. And a third endorses a more straightforward approach: claiming you were forced to borrow the books from an insistent friend.[2]

But best of all is the guileful yet effective tactic of corroding the spouse's defenses with gifts—albeit gifts of books. Lovingly present him or her with a handsome volume whenever you return from a bookstore foray, and the five or six other volumes you bought for yourself will slip through the defenses as byproducts of your largess.[3]

CHAPTER TEN

Fantasy Bookstore

To My Bookseller

Thou that mak'st gain thy end, and wisely well,

Call'st a book good, or bad, as it doth sell,

Use mine so, too; I give thee leave. But crave,

For the luck's sake, it thus much favour have,

To lie upon thy stall, till it be sought;

Not offered, as it made suit to be bought;

Nor have my title-leaf on posts, or walls,

Or in cleft-sticks, advanced to make calls

For termers, or some clerk-like serving-man,

Who scarce can spell th' hard names; whose knight less can.

If without these vile arts, it will not sell,

Send it to Bucklersbury, there 'twill well.[1]

BEN JONSON, THE AUTHOR OF THIS EPIGRAPH, was more than a brilliant seventeenth-century satiric playwright; he had book-marketing prescience as well. If his bookseller could not move his books without employing the vile promotional devices of his day, he wanted them dispatched to entrepreneurs who knew how to move a line—grocers. (Bucklersbury Street, incidentally, was to London grocers as Fleet Street was to London journalists.)

On Bucklersbury Street, *they*, at least, knew how to sell books. How prophetic Jonson was, for in today's world, every commercial enterprise from supermarkets to truck stops has bellied up to the book-trade bar. As incongruous as the scene may be, supermarket clientele do mix books with groceries: cantaloupes with Clancy, Stove Top with Steel, and they can throw in the collected works of that great woman of letters Britney Spears as well.

Supermarkets are not alone among the bookstore pretenders. Airports, train stations, department stores, card shops, churches, hardware stores, Kmarts, dimestores, truck stops, pharmacies—you name it, they all sell books.

Lewis Meyer, author of *The Customer Is Always* and former bookstore owner, fought this beast in his day: When a supermarket across the street stocked bookish delectations in the checkout line, he put canned peas in his front window; when a nearby drugstore began pumping Nancy Drew and the Hardy Boys, he stocked toothpaste and hot-water bottles.[2] Touché! he cried as he felt the saber point of commercial progress at his breast.

Meyer lost that battle. His successors in the book trade have lost the war. And we biblioholics, we idolizers of print and page, are much the worse for this diffusion of our end-all and be-all to every entre-preneur—bookish or otherwise—with the business chutzpah to know how to turn a buck. For people actually buy those express-lane volumes! Supermarkets are as far from a bona fide bookstore as Lynchburg is from Maryknoll, and people still buy books there. And that means trouble for the trade, not to mention us. Many book buyers, it seems, don't give a whit for ambience. They'll buy a book in an airport concourse as easily as they'll buy one from Blackwell's in Oxford.

Hence, the ignominious specter that dots our land—the bookstore supermarket: retail outlets that sell books much like convenience stores sell corn chips. Spanking clean businesses, as bright as a hospital operating room, with everything just so, offering only the latest squeaky-clean volumes hot off the presses, set off in antiseptic sixteen-copy floor displays surrounded by cardboard blurbissimo of a mawkish quality to make even the most egotistical author flush with shame—if that is possible. There are gewgaws and cumshaws on every shelf, and they sell cards and stationery and who knows what else. They have no feel, no atmosphere.

And we true-blue book bloods, we shake our heads in dismay. Oh, it is not much we ask of our passion. Our requirements for a bookstore are less than draconian. We only want a surfeit of titles, both ancient and contemporary. We require only the most cursory level of efficiency. We seek only a bookish ambience wherein the fusty odors of paper and ink are allowed to permeate every niche and nook. We seek leisure, time, comfort, atmosphere, the conviviality of our peers, and low prices. And we want all of this offered graciously *without* some sixteen-year-old naif shoving his or her freshly scrubbed face into our ambit and asking, "Can I help you?" every five minutes.

Laden with the incubus of the book disease, racked with guilt and angst over our profligate buying habits, we should be allowed to dream—of happy times, of buying unencumbered by the burdens we bear, of playing out our bookish fantasies in mental reverie. We dream of the perfect bookstore. We search far and wide to find it. When we blow into a new town, we scour the cityscape for something somewhere that lives up to our notion of proper bookselling. But the only place we find it is in our dreams. A mythical place somewhere in our imagination where the proprietor, genius that he or she is, has built an establishment designed solely to meet our bookish needs.

And what would this perfect bookstore be like? What would be its lineaments and habiliments? Its yin and yang?

We offer the following as a working model for any enterprising soul who doesn't necessarily want to hew to the laws of commercial success, but wants instead to give a lot of terminal biblioholics one last romp in elegiac book fields before adjourning this happy meeting called life.

GENERAL AMBIENCE

Rather than mandating where our mythical bookstore would be located, it is simpler by far to say where it should *not* be located. And that is, in a shopping center. The neon glare of an urban mall is not conducive to book browsing and buying. It's too bright, too clean, and too efficient. And it smells too good. Plus, the foot traffic is composed of, well, the hoi polloi. Not to sound elitist or anything, but the hoi polloi are not really our kind of people, especially when they shop for books. They have a lot of extraneous and unimportant things on their minds when they stroll into a mall bookshop. They want a birthday gift or an anniversary memento or a lurid page-turner for their great-nephew's singles' cruise to Mazatlan, or a big book—"a nice, big, *long* one"—for a relative bed-bound at the hospital. They just came from Penney's, they need to hit Walgreens and Circus World yet, and they're in a hurry to get it done and then get out. Very plebeian, very demotic, very, well, hoi-polloi-ish.

Biblioholism: The Literary Addiction

Needless to say, we biblioholics want and need more than that. Oh, we'll take it if it's all that is available—alcoholics don't need the bonhomie of an Irish pub to drink—but if given our druthers we'd like something that meets our needs. That is, a milieu, aged and dignified, where intellectuals lounge in bookish deportment, flipping though pages in calculated leisure. We want to overhear thought-provoking conversation spoken by erudite peers in convivial comity. This is not to suggest that it must be an oak-paneled sanctuary of learning with motes of dust dancing in sunbeams over a parquet floor—although that would be nice. For that matter, a golden dome and roving monks would be nice, too. All we seek is a place where we don't have to wear outfielders' flip-down shades to adjust to the high-frequency lights when we walk through the door. A little decay, a little character, a little feel. That's all.

The floors, of course, would be wood, creaking occasionally under our stride to give the place an old-world feel, and the books would be shelved, not in sterile portable racks but in floor-to-ceiling glory. The layout would be labyrinthine, with little hideaways jammed into every corner. Overstuffed chairs and sofas would dot the place and imbue it with a sense of leisure. It might provide its customers with seating autochthonous to the given disciplines—a pew in religion, old-fashioned desks in the kids' section, a shrink's couch in psychology. Provocative posters proclaiming quotes from famous writers would hang on the walls, and, of course, four-foot-high cardboard cutouts of Garfield or Snoopy would be noticeably absent. And, not least of all, it would have a bathroom—after all, we'll be spending the day there.

The perfect bookstore would not strive for 7-Eleven efficiency either. Why, we might even have to prowl toward the back room to find a clerk. Unhurried and unharried: that's how we shop for books.

INVENTORY

Tens and hundreds of thousands of volumes will stock our fantasy bookstore, all pulled neatly to the front of dark wood shelves, with sections set off discretely from each other in separate rooms with wide doorways. The sections would be arranged in a classical hierarchy, from Philosophy to Humor and everything between, including even the most esoteric subjects. There will never be a book that we want and they don't have. But, conversely, with every trip we'll find a book we didn't think anybody had.

And the stacking will make sense. Someone with a knowledge of each field will be specially brought in to arrange the books, someone for whom the words "Sociology/Religion," or "Popular Culture/Sociology," written on the back covers are redundant. Thus, Walker Percy's *The Moviegoer* would not be in the Film section. Martin Luther would not be on the Black Issues shelf, John Calvin wouldn't be in Fashion, *The Carpetbaggers* wouldn't be in Home Repair, Oral Roberts wouldn't be set alongside Oral Hygiene, and *Deliverance* wouldn't be in Religion.

A continual flow of stock is *de rigueur*, of course—even on the discount shelves—with the slow-movers sharing shelf space with the bestsellers. In the contemporary book world, even modern books are nowhere to be seen a year or two after publication. That is clearly unacceptable to us. So we would require about one-third of the store's inventory to have been in place since the store opened, with many titles on the shelves that nobody has ever asked about, or at most, only once every five or six years.

And *no* computer books. In fact, the perfect bookstore owner would not even be aware that the computer has been invented. This is, of course, a mildly technophobic view of things. But when we look at the unspeakable damage the computer revolution has wreaked on our language, with its bastardized jargon—"direct-connect modem," "top-down programming," etc.—and its insistence that nouns and adverbs perform unnatural acts on each other—"user-friendly," etc.—it seems woefully out of place in a store where language is revered. Besides, computers themselves are the harbinger of something that should, by the mere mention of it, make our scalps crawl—the paper-less society. Think of it: no books whatsoever! Just PCs and floppy disks and those little screens that beep a lot. There is something odious about the notion of hauling the laptop to the beach, punching up the latest Mary Higgins Clark, and enjoying a day in the sand. Something downright malevolent about sitting in a high-tech media center reading *The Shipping News* on a screen. No fingering the pages, no jotting notes in the margins, no tactile pleasure from feeling the book in our hands, no ink and paper smells. We get the biblioholic d.t.'s just thinking about it.

No, our fantasy bookstore will have no computer books. Computer types have their own stores. Let them go there.

BOOKSTORE PERSONNEL

What, then, of the bookseller, the dispensers of this thing we cannot live without, the seller of our drug? What manner of man or woman is this?

The perfect bookseller would operate his or her store for the sole purpose of being around books. As Edward Shils has written, a bookseller should be "somewhat daft in a socially useful and quite pleasant way but nonetheless off his head, to give himself to bookselling."[3]

The perfect bookseller would eat, drink, sleep, dream, and talk books. And during lunch hour he or she would read the *New York Times Book Review,* the *New York Review of Books,* and *Publishers Weekly*—a bookperson through and through, right down to the last synapse and corpuscle.

Booksellers should be so into the art of books that they, like dog owners, soon come to resemble their wares. Bibliophile Eugene Field's bookseller spent so much time rummaging in the corners of his shop "with folios and quartos and other antique tomes that he talked in black-letter and [had] the modest, engaging look of a brown old stout binding." The man also gave off an "odor of mildew and tobacco commingled, which is more grateful to the true bibliophile than all the perfumes of Araby."[4]

True, this intimates a conspicuous dearth of all things pragmatic in booksellers, but their other merits obviate any necessity of practicality. Einstein, for example, could not balance his checkbook. Ralph Waldo Emerson once cogitated deep and hard over whether to push a wheelbarrow or to pull it. Isaac Newton cut two holes in his study door, a large one for his cat, a small one for his kitten. Field knew philosophers who couldn't shoo chickens. And does anybody get in these luminaries' faces because they weren't practical? Of course not. The same goes for perfect booksellers. We don't want them to step out to our car and set the timing for us.

They're booksellers, not paragons of commerce. Their entry into the trade is something all biblioholics can relate to: at one point in life they probably became hooked on buying books, and—the logic here is singular to the addictive mentality—most likely they decided to sell books in order to make more money to buy more books. That's the attitude we want in a bookstore owner. The books themselves are the obsession, not moving them. Granted, this seems a lot to ask, as proprietors not obsessed with the profit-debit ledger will soon be ex-proprietors. But that's their problem, not ours. And besides, we're talking utopia here, not the real world.

Which brings us to bookstore clerks. The fact is, booksellers in today's world frequently make shortsighted hiring decisions. The famous Dr. Johnson book-throwing incident serves as an exemplary illustration. The eminent lexicographer once trundled into a London bookseller's shop seeking literary employment. After the seller, a man named Osborne, had given Johnson the once-over—the doctor was a girthy man with stubby fingers and a coarse face, and he dressed like a stevedore—Osborne dismissed him with the words "You would make a better porter." This enraged the good doctor. He picked up a folio and fired it at the bookseller's head, felling him. Then he stepped over the prostrate victim, while uttering the epithet "Lie there, thou lump of lead."[5]

While there are few, if any, Johnsons about these days—even fewer seeking bookstore employment—many booksellers seem to have abandoned the desire for bookish quality in their employees. One biblioholic recently stood impressed before the healthily endowed literature shelves of a bookstore and nonchalantly commented to a clerk who had meandered by, "You have a very good selection of classics here." To which the clerk responded, "Yeah, I guess so. The only one I've ever read was *Love Story*."

It may be true that young, intelligent, well-read, eclectic, savvy folks with PhDs who happily turn up their noses at lucrative careers in commerce to scrape in subsistence wages working weekends and nights in a bookstore do not even exist. But that's beside the point. We know we'd do it if we could.

It goes without saying that we don't want the disease that has infected the rest of the retail world to take root in our shrine of biblioholic consumption. This is not just any store; it is a *bookstore*. Thus, the virtues of retail commerce are mandatory: courtesy, friendliness, knowledge of the product, an attitude of service, and probably even name tags so we don't expend our erudition on some mooching passerby who simply stepped inside to copy a recipe out of Martha Stewart.

But there is more. The clerks must rise above the common issue in demeanor, attitude, and knowledge of the product. They should be, preferably, one of us. They must know our innermost workings, what makes us tick.

And if we were doing the interviews, what would be our criteria? Who would staff our perfect store? The perfect bookstore clerk would possess:

* * *

1. An extreme reluctance to rush up and ask, "Can I help you?" True biblioholics rarely need help, and if we do, we have it quite within our mental and linguistic powers to ask them. And it goes without saying that when we do ask, the clerk will not—as so many currently do— immediately tow us off to the obvious place in the shelves where the requested tome would likely be stacked. We may be addicts, but we are not stupid addicts. We've already looked *there*.

This does not mean, however, that we don't want them to talk to us. We do. Sometimes we are beside ourselves with desire to talk with them, if for no other reason than to show off how much we know about a given topic. And when we sidle up to their desk or counter with that glint of expatiation in our eyes and throw down the gauntlet of conversation in the form of some witty epithet or epigrammatic *bon mot*, we expect them to take it up. After all, we are on a high. We've got books under our arms, the flush of acquisition engulfs our bodies, and we want to talk about it. The clerk must be there as a willing codependent, to assure us of the happy times ahead, to underline the significance of the books we've purchased. In short, to pump us up.

2. Oracular wisdom. Not only must they be conversant on what's new, what's old, what's hot, and what's not (without consulting the bestseller list), they must also be able to field judiciously and without malice even the most imprecise query, like "I want something three hundred pages long with fully clothed people on the cover and lots of action but no violence, sex, or vulgarity for my friend who lives in a Trappist monastery." And then, if such a work exists, they would find it.

Or, the customer may know one important thing about the book—"It's blue"—but be ignorant of other details like title, author, publisher, and date, and the clerk would still be able to track down the book. Now certainly, we biblioholics would never pull such stunts;

we are too well read. But we would like to see our perfect bookstore clerks have sufficient grasp of the trade to deal with them.

3. A sure, deft, and personal knowledge of us as individuals. Many bookstore clerks, to their credit, already practice this courtesy; they know their customers by their interests. Thus, there are cat people, horse people, physics people, fitness freaks, self-help people, detective people, local history people, etcetera.

   But it happens all too infrequently. For most clerks we are faceless buying machines, deranged biblioholics who only want to sate our book-lust and get chummy with the personnel so that later when we hit the skids we can capitalize on that friendship and hit them with a request for credit—or even money. Hence, they quite naturally attempt to distance themselves. They don't comment on our purchases; they don't even engage us in conversation. In a perfect bookstore, the clerks wouldn't be like that.

   They would know each of us so well that if we said, "I want a light novel," they would be able to match our predilections in fiction with exactly the correct book. And they'd assume a sense of accountability, too. They would know that if we didn't like the book they chose, it would be their heinies. The mark of a perfect bookstore clerk is the sort of intimate knowledge that would allow them to choose our books for us. It rarely ever comes to that, of course, but it is something we expect.

* * *

THE USED-BOOK ROOM

And, of course, the perfect bookstore would also have a used-book section, a sort of bargain-basement emporium set off from the rest of the store where the ambience of that particular slice of the book trade is cultivated.

For used bookstores *are* different from new bookstores. A philosophy entirely foreign to the big supermarket bookstore is at play. Here, neatness is not a requisite. In fact, the used-book room in our perfect bookstore would of necessity be an absolute mess. Books on the shelves—all hardbound sans dust jackets—would be organized to suit the bookseller's whimsy, the lower shelves obscured by stacks of books on the floor. The clerk's desk, in fact, would not even be seen, so high the piles around it, and his or her head would appear as a mere cork floating on a sea of books.

And dust. Book dust has a context all its own. It is exceptionally vile. Used books can look deceptively clean, but spend a few hours handling them and you'll come out of that exercise looking like you just got off an eight-hour shift at a coal mine. And the smell—optimally, the used-book room would sink under a potent fog of mildewed paper and binding smell so thick a road-grader would have to be brought in simply to remove it.

Jumble, disorder, creaking wood floors, dust, a musty fog, perhaps even books stacked two deep on the shelves—these are the prerequisites to used book buying. They all point to one thing, the singular enticement that draws all to the used bookstore: a sense of discovery. For the biblioholic, the used bookstore holds treasures not known to spic-and-span retail operations. The old books we thought we'd never see, the books we'd never heard of on topics of interest, the out-of-print and hard-to-get varieties.

And once we've found one, we can open the cover and see small itsy-bitsy numbers like $3.00 and $5.00 on the top right corner of the flyleaf and know that even that number is open to negotiation.

Ah yes, but reality intrudes. Such a place does not exist. But we can dream, can't we?

CHAPTER ELEVEN

Reading

People say that life is the thing,
but I prefer reading.[1]

FOR THE ROMAN PLINY, no pleasure of life stood alongside reading in stature.[2] Poet Alexander Pope said he would rather be reading than talking.[3] And from Philip Hamerton we read: "When I open a noble volume, I say to myself, 'Now the only Croesus that I envy is he who is reading a better book than this.'"[4]

We biblioholics have been there. When push comes to shove, we'd rather be reading—than talking, than eating, than loving, than working, than playing, than shopping, than doing anything except, perhaps, buying books. To us, nirvana is retreating to the isolation of a favorite chair, where, surrounded by the accoutrements of the craft— the bright light, the noshables, etc.—we thumb the good tome in our laps. And if life could be lived sixteen hours a day in a cushy chair, we'd let the heavens resound in a chorus of praise.

But such is not our lot. We have to work, travel, eat, visit friends, and perform all sorts of mundane duties that have the potential to rob us of precious reading time. The easy comfort of our favorite chair is simply a best-case scenario.

Biblioholics must read wherever and whenever possible, and even when it doesn't seem possible. Why else do we drag a book along with us wherever we go? There is absolutely no time or place unsuitable for cracking a volume and indulging our passion. In trains, planes, buses, cars, and all other transport; at meals, in bed, on the john, at work, in dentists' offices, in supermarket checkout lines—wherever—we hold true to our biblioholic calling: *we read*. If our car breaks down on the freeway, we merely reach across the seat and pull out a volume. When our barber finally tires of occupational small talk, we flip open the magazine on our laps. After we get comfy on the chair lift, we reach into our parka and pull out a book.

It matters not where or when. We must read. John Wesley read history, philosophy, and poetry while riding his horse, sometimes one hundred miles a day.[5] Lawrence of Arabia read Aristophanes in the original while on camelback traveling through Arabia.[6] William Archer, a London operagoer, at one particular performance slept "through almost the entire performance, waking up in the intervals to draw from his pocket and peruse a volume of Gibbon's 'Decline and Fall.'"[7]

But there are settings and times when practiced addicts must ply their craft with some expertise. There is rhyme and reason to bedtime reading, for example. There's more to restaurant reading than merely toting in a volume and cracking it while the chef does his thing in the back. We just don't dump a few volumes into the can and let it go at that. There's art involved.

What follows, then, is a guidebook to reading in a biblioholic's favorite haunts.

READING IN RESTAURANTS

Wise people have said that eating itself is an art that tolerates no rivals. The aromatic ambience, the delectable insertion of fork into mouth, the gratifying mastication, the savors that linger on the taste buds—all comprise an entity unto itself, it is said, so rewarding as to occupy totally one's senses.

For biblioholics, however, eating is just chewing and swallowing—so much time wasted on gratifying the baser senses. We do not live by bread alone. We must be reading, too. That goes for our meals at home—this is given—but it applies in spades to our dining out.

Reading in restaurants comes down to us laden with tradition. One conjures up visions of Papa, seated with pen and book in hand at some Parisian cafe, somehow managing to consume entire days at one table, drinking wine and rum and absinthe in such purported quantities that a normal person's liver would have upped and walked out of the place somewhere around noon. And he never got the bum's rush from any fractious restaurateurs, either.

Indeed, there is something about reading in a restaurant that is borderline romantic. Leaning back in that corner booth, an evocative title in our hands, a stale cup of java in front of us, every so often bolting forward to jot a phrase onto the napkin, we look like, well, poets—unknown belletrists scraping through the hardscrabble years and awaiting the distinction that is imminent. The waiter or waitress refills our cup, we drop a memorable apothegm or two, share a laugh fraught with meaning, scope out the joint, and return to our tome. Nonbiblioholics strain to espy our title; conversation is struck up on things Kafkaesque and Kierkegaardian; and we forge a genuine biblioholic simpatico with all around.

Reading

But we are not Papa. We are not changing the face of literature with our spare and truly true prose. We aren't lounging in some estaminet on the Rue Notre-Dame-des-Champs with Ford and Ezra and Scott and Zelda and Miss Stein. And we probably can't hold nearly as much of anything as Papa could, not even coffee.

No, if we want to eat and read in today's world, we're probably at the counter of Denny's or some such coffee shop—where else can we sit without being shooed out the door after a half hour?—surrounded by nonreaders in Kenworth caps who don't give a whit whether we're reading Margaret Drabble or Norman Drabble, while cryptic orders like "Two cluckers looking up with oink-meat squashed" serve as literate oases in a desert of guttural monosyllabic converse. And if that's not bad enough, they give us our check as they serve the meal.

Restaurant reading is not what it used to be. We can't kill half a day dominating a booth and drinking coffee or whatever else. We actually have to eat something.

And that poses big problems for us. Never mind the condemnatory or incriminatory words we may receive from other diners. You know what they're thinking, don't you, when they see some solitary soul march into a restaurant with book under arm? It's not, "My, what an interesting person. Must be very smart and very creative." On the contrary, it's: "What sort of social leper must resort to reading while seated in a public place consuming food? What kind of obsessed maniac can't take a few minutes out of his or her life to ingest victuals in peace?" We must be inured to this stuff. After all, we're biblioholics; we get it all the time. Our primary concern is logistics. Look at it this way: There's a book, there's a knife and a fork, there's a plate, and there's only so much table space. And we have only two hands.

How do we place our book in an accessible location on the table and make it stay open while wielding our cutlery? That's the real problem. Most biblioholics place the sugar dispenser on one side of the open book, although in pancake houses it is commonplace to use a syrup container. But syrup containers being what they are—that is, more syrup on the outside than on the inside—this can make future readings difficult, unless you turn pages with an acetylene torch. And with all that, we're still talking maybe forty-five minutes max of reading time.

Pizza joints are perhaps the premier locale for the restaurant-reading biblioholic these days, made more desirable since the invention of the deep-dish pizza. These dishes usually require a full thirty minutes' cooking time. And the Parmesan cheese shaker holds the pages down quite well in most cases.

However, some biblioholics are sensitive about their books' spines, not wanting them creased by a heavy cylinder of glass with grated cheese in it. A good motto to operate under in these conditions is "A book for the wait, a mag for the plate." When the pizza arrives, switch reading material.

A similar, more risky, venue for reading is the bar. Reading in bars is fraught with innumerable dangers. There's the poor lighting, the beer-soaked table, the continuous parade of foot traffic, the band, and the very good chance that a dropped book will become stuck for all time to one of those disgusting bar carpets.

Serious biblioholics are not swayed by such factors, however. They read regardless. J. A. Symonds enjoyed nothing more than "to sit in a bar room among peasants, carters, and postillions, smoking with a glass of wine beside him, and a stiff work" in front of him.[8] Holbrook Jackson recounts seeing one Cecil Chesterton "standing in the middle of a crowded London tap-room with a tankard of ale in one hand and a book in the other, chuckling over the page, unconscious of the din and reek of the place."[9]

READING ON THE TOILET

Back in the old days, toilet activity encompassed all of hygiene and even getting dressed. The toilet was the scene of much bewigged and beribboned social intercourse, as anyone who has seen the movie *Dangerous Liaisons* can attest to. Glenn Close and John Malkovich seemed to spend hours clowning around with their clothes, powdering their faces and wigs, and pulling on the strings and belts of those prom dresses and frilly tuxes that passed for daily knockabout attire to such an extent that the pressure inside their bodies had to be about a million psi. One more tug, it seemed, and Glenn Close would have gone up like Czechoslovakian plastique.

In the movie, they weren't reading anything at the time, but that's the exact place many of the ancient bookophiles got a lot of their input. Our forebears really knew how to use every moment of their time for reading; they had that problem wired. Rarely did they waste a minute's time while in the grooming process, or getting dressed, or performing all the necessary acts a person of good hygiene must undertake. They read while shaving and had their janissaries read to them while tugging on those Louis XIV outfits they always wore. One learned German even had Homer printed on india rubber so he could read it while in the tub.[10]

But in today's world, when we speak of toilet reading, we mean only one thing: reading while on the throne. We lack the domestic help to feed us with book knowledge while we put on our makeup or scrape the stubble off our faces, and the only other time during the whole toiletry ordeal that we have our hands entirely free is when we're actually sitting on the can.

The big question in all biblioholics' minds thus becomes: What is proper intellectual fare for this undertaking? What kinds of books do we have sitting next to the john (in addition to *The Water-Method Man*, of course, John Irving's novel about a guy who drank a great deal of water to help him with urination problems)?

In olden times the reading matter was, although quite frivolous for its day, pretty heavy-duty stuff in our terms: Zola's *Nana*, *The Golden Ass* of Apuleius, and the *Works* of the Marquis de Sade all appeared on the toilet table of one painting of an earlier era.[11] Today, our toilets are equipped with such intellectual food as compendia of salacious jokes and tomes examining various indiscreet bodily functions (perhaps the most highbrow being *Who Cut the Cheese: A Cultural History of the Fart*). But as the Romans used to say, *De gustibus non est disputandum*, or, on a more practical note, as we used to aver in my high school Latin class, *Semper ubi sub ubi*, which, while something of a nonsequitur, seems like good advice regardless of time, place, or book in hand.

READING IN BED

Reading in bed, as we all know, is a *sine qua non* of biblioholism. The bed, the covers, the sheets, the supine posture, the proximity of sweet surrender—it all puts us of a mind to read and think. As Eugene Field wrote, "All good and true book-lovers practise the pleasing and improving avocation of reading in bed."[12]

Implicit to bedtime reading, however, is the very real question of motivation. What is our rationale for reading in the sack? Do we read in bed to allow our minds gradually to drift from a state of complete sensual awareness, with brain activity at full-out levels, to the narcoleptic spaciness of presomnolent nods and then the final euphoric transition into full semiconsciousness? Or do we read to stay awake? In many respects, this is the litmus test of biblioholism. After all, sleep is the enemy! When we are sleeping, we allow our bodies to regenerate the energy needed to face a new dawn, true. But we are not reading.

Biblioholic John Collings Squire offers his equals in addiction sage advice: "Let sleep go," he wrote. "Let the morrow's duties go. . . . The bedside book for me is the book that will longest keep me awake."[13]

And, not only that, the hard-core biblioholic will make *sure* he or she doesn't drift off to dreamland. We contemporaries are mere dilettantes in this area, with our No-Doz, our three gallons of coffee that looks and tastes like it has just been drained from the crankcase of a Peterbilt diesel, our alternate hot and cold showers—it's all strictly soft-core stuff. Undiluted milquetoast. Eventually sweet slumber's beckoning will be heeded, eventually the rack will win out over the book every time, and off into the semiconscious netherworld we will fly—probably all too willingly. Put simply, when it's time to sleep, we sleep.

But our ancestors in addiction—now there were some folks who were serious about reading in bed. No price was too great to pay for the extra hour of wakefulness. Noted Chinese scholar Liu Hsun would often read all night and, in case the nods would attack, he rigged up a "lighted twist of hemp arranged in such a way as to burn his hair if he began to nod from drowsiness."[14] Another Chinese, Sun Ching, tied his hair to a beam overhead to prevent him from dozing off.[15] And a man named Ringelbergins slept transversely across two boards so that the discomfort would wake him in the night and allow his return to his books.[16]

Book studs nonpareil, that's what these literary Rambos were. Unfortunately, weaker biblioholics look at the question differently. They read to go to sleep. Books become soporifics. Best in this regard, of course, are erudite tomes filled with convoluted sentences and sesquipedalic prose, like a technical treatise on structural chemistry, or the writings of Henry James (a personal preference), which have the distinct somnolescent quality of containing absolutely no action. All that getting up in the morning, all that getting dressed, all the demure meetings, all those stilted drawing-room conversations, all that sitting around the dinner table acting hoity-toity, all those subtle nuances, and all those sentences with an average of forty-five prepositional phrases in each—within a page or two of reading the lids droop, the head clouds, the arms go weak, the book slides onto the floor, and it takes 4,500 amps of direct current shock to get you to the light switch without falling catatonic onto the floor.

Which brings up a crucial, soporific bed-book caveat: Do not employ the extremely large book for this purpose. A two-by-three-foot retrospective on Rubens or Rembrandt propped up daintily on your chest can, at the moment of surrender, fall with concussive impact onto your head or, at the very least, give you the feeling that somebody's just cut the air hose of your diving bell at two hundred meters.

READING WHILE TRAVELING

Books and traveling. There's something about the clickety-clack of the rails underfoot, something about the jet engines idling and the evacuation procedures being recited, that simply begs us to unsheath a volume and dive into it, bar cars and in-flight movies notwithstanding. (Except, of course, if we are traveling by Greyhound bus. There, reading is not the priority, surviving is.)

It's always been so. Napoleon, for example, fitted his coach with a shelf of books.[17] Pliny the Elder traveled about Rome in a sedan chair to ensure no interruption of his intellectual pursuits.[18] Many of Thomas Babington Macaulay's prodigious reading feats were accomplished while on board a ship.[19] In the salad days of the American railroad, both Hawthorne and Dickens commented on the great number of Americans who read while traveling.[20] And Julius Caesar, no slouch of a biblioholic, took great pains to ensure his books' safety while traveling, once swimming with "a book in one hand, a sword in the other,"[21] although it is unknown whether he was also reading at the time.

True biblioholics even read while employed in the most rudimentary form of transportation. They step beyond Charles Lamb's personal credo "When I am not walking, I am reading,"[22] and they stick a book in front of their faces even while strolling the busy metropolitan thoroughfares. Some even stick it too close. The eminent Dr. Johnson, nearsighted *in extremis*, shoved a volume right up to his eyes as he walked, "stepping over shadows and stumbling over sticks and stones."[23] Another great biblioholic, Thomas Hearne, often read while walking, and on several occasions when daylight had faded and he finally pulled his nose out of the volume, found himself totally lost.[24]

Other walking readers had more success. Macaulay could weave in and out of foot traffic with the élan of a messenger bicyclist when on London's congested streets, "walking as fast as other people walked, and reading a great deal faster than anybody else could read."[25] But then

Macaulay was in a class by himself: he could skim a book faster than normal people could turn pages.

Today, a fondness for reading while traveling does not necessarily mean one is a biblioholic. On the contrary, everybody—even those technocrats and number-crunchers whose lives are epitomized by flowcharts and quarterly statements—associates traveling with reading. Once the "Fasten Seat Belts" sign is off and the tray tables come down, all eyes are moving left to right across the page. There's something about all that time wasted, time when they could be making deals or playing with their Macintoshes, that prompts them to do *something*. So they read.

But what are they reading? That's the question. The in-flight magazine, a periodical encased in plastic, the evacuation procedures, some bestseller that beckoned from behind the mint display at the airport bric-a-brac shop? Right. The fact that they're reading is an exception, an exigency forced onto them, kind of like an art snob having to sit through a tractor pull because cousin Clive is in town for the weekend.

We biblioholics are a cut above this plebeian throng. We bring a book with us, probably several. I know of one biblioholic who walks onto airplanes dragging a briefcase the size of a Toyota Camry. None of those sleek attaché cases for him. It usually takes two flight attendants to help him heft the thing up to the bin. After all, there is a larger question at play here: How many is enough? Are two dozen paperbacks going to stay one's mind for two solid weeks at the in-laws, when even a day at the beach requires at least three? Can one book delight and satisfy for two or three long hours in the sky? What if we experience a mood swing as the plane encounters engine trouble in midflight and want to switch to something more practical—like the Twenty-third Psalm? (Not all of us possess the pertinacity—not to mention the *sangfroid*—of one biblioholic who, when her plane prepared for an emergency landing because of an engine fire, continued to plow headlong through the interminably boring first hundred pages of *The Magic Mountain* because it was something she wanted to do before she died.)

One book is never enough. Biblioholics always carry with them a portable library for traveling. This presents us with a different problem, though: packing. Those of us with the misfortune to have married a nonbiblioholic know exactly how this shakes out. When it comes to packing for a trip, that spouse of ours probably consumes four hours packing—three hours and fifty-eight minutes of which are taken up in handpicking individual socks, shirts, undergarments, pants, pantsuits, three-piecers, shoes, overcoats, boots, and all other garments known to man or woman. And over each item, he or she meditates more deeply and probingly than Congress trying to cut an entitlement program. Then during the last two minutes of the packing regimen, he or she nonchalantly tosses in a book or two, as a sort of lagniappe. We biblioholics have different priorities. We've got all our clothes in our suitcase in two minutes flat, and then we spend three hours and fifty-eight minutes deciding which books to bring.

READING AT WORK

The great bugaboo of all biblioholics is work. To be sure, we wouldn't do it if we didn't have to. However, not all of us can aspire to the schedule of poet Percy Shelley, who frequently spent sixteen hours a day reading.[26] No, we have to grind away the primo reading hours of every day while slaving under the thumb of some hard-edged tyrant who has as much sympathy for our biblioholic plight as do the leading mullahs of Iran for the artistic sensibilities of Salman Rushdie.

And why? To make money. And why do we need money? That's simple: To buy more books to read.

Oh, bring back the old days. There were more literary sugar daddies in those days than there were readers, all of whom were more than willing to dole out a living to some cosseted bibliophile who was to ingest all of the knowledge known to humanity and occasionally regurgitate it in some sort of pamphlet or poem. They called it patronage. In reading of these great bookmen of times past, a fact jumps out at you right from the get-go: None of them had day jobs. They were the Ward Cleavers of the eighteenth century. Every city seemed to lay claim to a set of gentrified Brahmin who did nothing but hunker down in some tavern somewhere and discourse on the books they'd read. James Boswell is forever expatiating on how he and Dr. Johnson and Oliver Goldsmith and David Garrick and other personages of the day, famous and obscure alike, did nothing all day but sit and read, sit and eat, sit and tell stories, and sit and drink.

Or, take the monks, those anchorites nonpareil, holed up in some twelfth-century monastery, food and board all part of the package, with nothing to do but consume their every waking hour absorbed in books. Sure, there were *some* inconveniences—strolling barefoot along cloistered halls with no central heating, sleeping on boards, forcing down some horrendous gruel three times a day, depriving themselves of all creature comforts, undergoing self-inflicted austerity that had no peer, waking up every two hours to pray, wearing those coarse hooded outfits that would take the skin off their faces like a Black & Decker high-powered sander if they got too close. But look at the perks! All that time for reading.

Reading

But we—we have to punch some clock and kowtow to some upper-management bureaucrat who doesn't know Sam Johnson from Magic Johnson and who thinks James Boswell is a former outside linebacker for the Seattle Seahawks with a punk hairdo. And then, if we bring our biblioholism to the workplace and pursue it only during the legally mandated breaks and lunchtime—in short, whenever our overlords permit—everybody else in the plant looks at us like we're some kind of weirdo.

It's almost as if society in our day of multimedia communication has something against us bookophiles. Our coworkers get us around the coffeepot or the copy machine and replay the great moments of the local sports teams' nightly games, recount every poignancy of the previous evening's episode of *Law and Order*, or discourse in the discombobulated metalanguage of computer programming. And if we can't pull our weight in the conversation, they peer down their noses at us as if we rank just below plankton on the food chain. When we try to be sociable and discuss something we're interested in with these philistines, they give us a look like we're not fit to breathe free air.

Work—as Holden Caulfield posited about many things in life—is a royal pain in the nates (my translation).

But we have ways, fellow sufferers, we have ways. It's called reading on the job, and it is only for the brazen among us, those of us who have cultivated the near-telepathic sixth sense of anticipating our bosses' and fellow laborers' prying eyes and probing questions before they spring them on us. Integral to our success, of course, is the ability to hide the books we are reading. There are basically three time-tested techniques for reading at work, all of which can be extremely dangerous to the bindings—not to mention our jobs:

* * *

1. Hiding the book under papers while reading on the top of our desk. This technique precludes any sense of neatness and order you may possess. If you are the type who religiously corrals paper clips and sticks them into those little magnetic cups; if your middle desk drawer looks like you hired somebody to come in and arrange your pens and pencils; if you're on the phone to personnel complaining vehemently when the trashman is so much as five minutes late making his rounds; if you find yourself on your hands and knees every once in a while digging used staples out of the carpet; if you feel the inexorable urge to clear your desk and wipe it down with industrial-strength Lysol every two hours, forget it. You can't pull this trick off. Camouflage is of the utmost, and the more papers and computer printouts you have strewn around your desktop, the better.

   Make a small hole the size of one book page in the debris directly in front of you, place the desired tome within it, and transfer a mass of papers alternately back and forth, covering the verso page, then the recto, then the verso, etc., as you read. Always scope out the area before changing pages.

2. Laying the book on your lap directly beneath your middle desk drawer. The disaster-area desktop is not compulsory for this technique, although various reports must be placed directly in front of you to complete the pose. As a boss or coworker approaches your desk, merely pull your chair up quickly into the chair well and make like you are

crunching numbers or doing whatever it is that you do. But remember: the hands must be placed on the desktop at all times to remove suspicion.

3. Placing the book open inside the middle desk drawer. This is perhaps the riskiest of the three because the rapid pulling up of the chair into the chair well is always accompanied by the cacophonous slamming of the desk drawer, which can give rise to managerial interrogation. All other aspects are identical to the book-on-lap technique.

* * *

It also works to secrete books within stacks of reports when en route to the copy machine, there placing, oh, maybe two thousand pages into the automatic feed and simulating hand-collating on the top while actually reading the book of the day beneath that detritus of disheveled papers. This works simply because dominating the copy machine for two or three hours with megareport reproduction is an American business tradition. No one apart from management has the sand to question you.

Also, reading while standing at a file cabinet—again, laying out two or three reams of reports and computer printouts for camouflage—offers the additional advantage of seeing bosses and coworkers approaching over those insidious and dehumanizing cubbyhole walls so many companies insist on erecting. Thus, no surprises. Plenty of time for cover-up.

Alas, for you biblioholic computer operators, there seems to be no hope in sight. Unless you avail yourselves of e-books, you will actually have to work.

READING AT A NONBIBLIOHOLIC'S HOUSE

Here we broach the delicate topic of social etiquette. Sensitive biblioholics consider their image when they visit other people's homes. They worry lest their host think less of them when they arrive at the door hauling a book or two. They agonize whether it is outré to crack their book and start reading the moment the host launches into that interminable brattle about office politics or the summer trip to the in-laws'.

But those are the sensitive ones. Real biblioholics obviate all such concerns by simply striding in the front door, hieing to the nearest chair, and planting themselves, with book on lap, for the duration.

A word is perhaps warranted here about sociability in general. Consider the style of life we have carved out for ourselves. As obsessive readers we live in self-imposed ostracism. We hole up somewhere, start reading, and the world as we know it ceases to exist. I am reminded here of the story of one ancient biblioholic, Budaeus, a philologist, who happened to be reading in his study when his house caught on fire. A servant rushed in to warn him, and he curtly dispatched the footman by saying, "Tell my wife: you know that I never interfere with the household," and continued with his book.[27]

We are mini-Budaeuses. Once we open a tome, all sense of time and place flies. We and our book become metaphysically one, impervious to outside stimuli. We sit as insensate blobs, sequestered, cloistered, holed up in some corner—just us, our thoughts, and a book.

Some nonbiblioholics, unaware of the intricacies of the disease, read these signs and mistakenly think we're lonely. They invite us to dinner parties or over for a social evening; they put on a sumptuous spread and a happy face and do everything in their power to make us feel wanted and unlonely. They don't know the position that puts us in, the tough choices it offers us. Because we will read. And when they see us playing out our passion, they don't know what to do. Throw us out, scold us, bring our dinner to us, bond with us, have a sharing time, or what.

Some benighted souls, despite all the signals we transmit, may even pursue the matter. They may keep trying to talk to us. Bless their hearts, they're only trying to be sociable; they're only holding to some punctilio of common courtesy. We can't blame them for that. They just don't know what it is like.

As an effective method to ward off this particular inroad into our reading habits, I suggest the following:

* * *

1. Don't look up from your book. Under no circumstances establish eye contact. Mere nonacknowledgment will drive away the sensitive host. If this fails, a raised hand indicating that the speaker should stop might work.

2. However, if the host persists, use the following comments as the situation dictates:

    "Did you hear anything? I thought I heard somebody talking."

    "How am I supposed to concentrate on this book while you're talking to me?"

    "I love this sentence so much I've been reading it over and over since you came in."

    "You're right in my light."

Taken in concert with definitive body language, such comments should do the trick.

* * *

163

But an obsession to read at all times and places is but one of the troubling symptoms of biblioholism. We now move to the area of book protection, a fertile area of the disease where paranoia reigns supreme and biblioholic symptoms are on garish display.

CHAPTER TWELVE

To Stack and Protect

Keep your Books behind stout

Gratings, and in no wise let

any Person come at them to take

them from the Shelf except Yourself.[1]

SO, YOU'VE COME THIS FAR in this book, and maybe you're thinking, "I don't have it so bad. I read a lot, sure, and I buy quite a few books. But this biblioholism doesn't seem like the bummer this guy is making it out to be." Yes, the doubts may be burrowing back into your cranium, that insidious dubiety that marks all diseases of an addictive nature. You may be having second thoughts about whether you even have a problem.

Don't be ashamed of it. Denial is such a potent force; it gallops unreined through all stages of the disease. Why, I knew a biblioholic once who, in the later stages of the disease, housed his library in what was tantamount to a germ-free environment. I was immediately rendered suspicious by the videocameras mounted in the ceiling, the frisking conducted upon entrance to and departure from his holy of holies, and the little proctologists' gloves I had to wear just to get into the place. It seemed a little extreme, but, as we all know, some people can be serious book aficionados without slipping over the edge. Human compassion prompted me to give him every benefit of the doubt before subjecting him to my Nathan-like finger of accusation.

But it was the meteorological equipment that gave him away. He had it on sound advice that the optimal temperature for book storage was sixty-five degrees Fahrenheit, with a relative humidity of between 45 and 50 percent and with, of course, absolutely no exposure to sunlight. And he had installed a weather station to monitor it. A double-recording thermograph stood on a table in the corner; numerous miniature pyrheliometers, which sang out like Lamborghini car alarms whenever a single beam of sunshine penetrated their hyper-sensitive glass globes, were placed strategically about the room; and every half hour or so Armando—his curator!—would whip out a sling psychrometer and twirl it around his head for a few seconds to take a relative humidity reading. The guy didn't have a hardbound book in the place, yet he carried on like he was trustee for a roomful of Gutenberg Bibles. He had a *serious* problem.

I confronted him with tough love, and he leveled me in his sights, his face assuming the sort of mien a speed-limit driver assumes when espying a pizza delivery car hot on his bumper in his rearview mirror, and said, "Problem? I don't have a problem."

Denial can strike at any time. There is no sanctuary, no harbor of refuge where we can escape its wicked grasp. This fellow had it bad, yet in his own eyes he was merely a normal guy who loved books.

As for you, it's gut-check time. Time to get right down to the real nitty-gritty. For nowhere within the malevolent course of this disease do the symptoms manifest themselves as they do in the area of book care. How do you stack your books? How do you handle them? What sorts of precautions do you exercise before showing them or lending them? For as much as we can kid ourselves, we do not buy them just to read them. If that were so, we would spend all of our time at the public library. Pride of possession is a powerful biblioholic motivator.

Of course, not all biblioholics are fastidious neatniks who consume hours in sorting and stacking their books. Neatness is not a prerequisite of the disease per se. Many of the old timers were A numero uno slobs, and yet no one would contest their inclusion in the biblioholic hall of shame.

Thomas de Quincey, for example, simply piled books in his study until all that was navigable was a narrow path from desk to fireplace, and another from fireplace to door. But he knew where everything was. Servants tidying up the place were dismissed as vandals. And when his stock grew too large for four walls, he did the expedient thing: he locked the door and set up shop in another room.[2]

Many other biblioholics of times past were inveterate slobs as well. One Lord de Tabley left so many books lying around that his servant looked upon them as "personal enemies."[3] And of course, the infamous Boulard, with his seven *houses* full of books, was not overly concerned with the protocols of attractive display. He was meshuga.

Most biblioholic tendencies, however, run the other way—toward neatness. There's something about handling our books, about arranging them just so, that simply turns us on. We are forever lolling around our bookshelves, first pulling a book out, then sticking it back in, aligning them with the front of the shelf, and shifting them from shelf to shelf to make room for new additions.

And we classify them: alphabetical by author; divided by subject matter; in a Dewey Decimal System with or without the numbers; by publisher; chronologically by date of publication; by size—big ones below, little ones on top; by number of pages—thick to thin or thin to thick; by country of origin; by most liked to least liked; by read and unread; by color—from white to black or vice versa; by number of pictures; or by whatever criteria we find interesting at the moment.

Now it may strike some that people engaging in this sort of ritual would be well advised to get a life. But there is more. Classifying and sorting is a mentality common to acquisitive addiction of all types. We like to handle them; we like their feel on our fingertips, their heft in our hands. Much of this satisfaction is natural, endemic to the more benign pleasures of owning objects of any kind. But many book-handling practices are also quite troubling, serious signs that one has gone over the edge.

When, we ask, have we passed through the suburbs of sanity? When have we gone too far in our penchant for stacking and protecting our books? Consider the following three criteria:

*   *   *

1. Arranging them by color is one thing. Rebinding them in various colors, as is done in some famous museums, is another, more disconcerting, trait. If your books sport distinctive colors, say, black for theology, light brown for medicine, light green for math and physics, dark green for poetry, etc., as is done at the Bodleian,[4] you have a problem. Some have taken it even further: Oscar Wilde had Dorian Gray bind nine copies of one book in nine different colors to "suit his different moods."[5] Louis XV's daughters each had a library bound in a separate color.[6]

2. If you decide to bind your books in human skin, then you should seek immediate professional help. While, it is true, biblioholics have often sought strange media for binding their beloved treasures—in everything from rattlesnakes and crocodiles to hogskin (especially suitable for the works of Francis Bacon) and a pair of buckskin breeches worn exclusively in a circumnavigation of the globe and thereafter immortalized as the binding of a book[7]—binding them in human skin steps over the line. Not only is it sick and demented, but it poses practical problems. The hair is tough to get rid of, for one thing. And for another, some skin is simply not suitable for binding—consider a book bound in Manuel Noriega's face, for example. But biblioholics have resorted to this perverted practice in times past. Thomas Carlyle once commented that "the French nobles laughed at Rousseau's theories, but that their skins went to bind the second edition of his book."[8] And one romantic Russian poet, seeking to impress a lady, bound his sonnets in the skin of his amputated leg.[9]

3. Shelf maintenance. How serious are you about shelving? You know you've gone too far if you affix little signs to each shelf identifying the subject matter: "Sociology," for example, or authors' names, "Amis, Kingsley—Dos Passos, John." A Dewey Decimal System also gives cause for concern. And you know you are a total no-hoper if at the entrance to your library you provide visitors with a map of your stacks. Other particularly worrisome signs are the possession of a two- or three-tiered rolling cart, as

used in libraries and bookstores, to wheel your books to their proper places in the stacks, or library-style ladders to reach the topmost shelves. These would be harbingers for book trouble ahead.

* * *

Which brings us to bookmarks. How particular are you about bookmarks? If you are, you may be in danger. Nonbiblioholics usually don't care how they mark their books—with pencils, rulers, paper clips, razor blades, tab tops, combs, slices of American cheese, kippered herring, beef jerky, drinking straws, bread crusts, strips of bacon—in short, anything within arm's reach. One ancient bookman named Selden employed his eyeglasses for this purpose. In fact, he purchased them by the gross because he also happened to be quite absentminded. After his library was bequeathed to the Bodleian, it was common for readers to pull books from the shelves and find a pair of spectacles falling out.[10]

Some nonbiblioholics mark their places by laying the book face down on a table. Others run a rubber band around the book, and others still engage in the maddening habit of turning over the corners of the pages. Insisting on the use of thin bookmarks only, or even a single slip of paper—preferably acid-free—is one of the telling signs of biblioholism.

The matter of insertions is also relevant here. Have you ever pulled a friend's book off the shelf, opened it, and been inundated by a complete New England autumn that came fluttering to the floor in the form of pressed leaves? You probably don't have to worry about that friend. Leaves, notes, letters, copies of magazine articles, locks of hair— these are all biblioholic no-no's.

And what about admittance to the library per se? Do you get a little squeamish when the Great Unwashed descend on your library en masse with their yahoo book-handling ways? Does it bother you just a little bit when some guy rolls up one of your high quality paperbacks like a supermarket tabloid and takes off after flying insects? What about that lady with the runny nose who spends a half hour flipping through your first-edition Hemingway? Or that rube who is forever setting a sweaty glass on your coffee-table book? Or those bumpkins who wave your books around like a conductor's baton during animated conversation? How about those little grand-kids who, shortly after being allowed a few minutes' frolic in your library, are apprehended playing tic-tac-toe on the title page of your first-edition Willa Cather? Thinking about things like this sends biblioholics into apoplectic seizures. Book fiends are moved to all manner of measures to protect their beloved books—even to the point of seriously considering the question of allowing others to enter their library at all.

Biblioholics of time past were more than a little paranoid in this area. For example, nobody saw the great biblioholic Heber's vast store-house until after the guy was dead.[11] Eugene Field summed up the attitude well in this little ditty:

> Oh, I should bind this priceless prize
> In bindings full and fine,
> And keep her where no human eyes
> Should see her charms, but mine![12]

This is where we biblioholics are coming from. Admit it. It would be nice to install a buzzer-activated door to our library. It would make us a lot happier if we equipped our library with wall-length, one-way mirrors, behind which we could sit in unseen surveillance, a Doberman at our side. It would be nice to hire our own rent-a-cops or even to require all visitors to dress up in Bekins moving suits before we let them in.

It would be terrific to put our severe wackiness about books on public display. But most of us simply won't do it—most of us want to continue with some semblance, however tenuous, of a social life. So sensitive biblioholics quash their baser instincts and take a more moderate tack. They educate visitors as to proper book care; they set a shining example by handling their books like icons when visitors are near. Some have even gone so far as to post a list of book-handling rules on the wall of their library.

One such list of rules follows.

* * *

"The Book Handler's Ten Commandments"

ALL VISITORS shall show respect for the holy ground of this library by removing their shoes immediately upon entrance.

ALL PENS and other writing utensils shall be checked at the door.

BEFORE HANDLING a book, thou shalt cleanse thy hands in the bowl of rosewater provided at the door.

AFTER CLEANSING thy hands, thou shalt don a pair of the little plastic gloves, also provided at the door.

To Stack and Protect

THOU SHALT NOT GRAB a book by the top of the spine when removing it from the shelf. Rather, said book shall be handled as one handles a Ming Dynasty vase—with both hands.

THOU SHALT NOT BREATHE, spit, sneeze, cough, drool, or discharge sputum of any type in the direction of a book.

ALL WHO MARK a page by turning down a corner in any of these books, or even think about doing so, shall immediately be escorted to the guillotine in the garage.

ALL WHO WISH to turn pages in a book must use the specially made paper knives provided at the end of each stack.

ALL WHO WET their finger to turn a page shall die a quick and immediate death by strangling.

YE WHO CREASE a spine shall immediately report to the owner of this library, who shall crease thy skull.

* * *

However, perhaps the most effective strategy of all is one described by A. Edward Newton in his essay "On Forming a Library." Newton tells of a friend who owned a famous collection of poetry—Wordsworth, Byron, Keats, Browning, et al.—in their original bindings. He loved these books and was not of a mind to subject them to the philistine hordes, so when visitors descended on him, he removed a small key from his pocket, pointed to a case in the corner, and said something to the effect of "You know poetry is my strong point; here is the key to that bookcase yonder: be very careful, but enjoy my books to your heart's content." And regardless of the crimes these visitors committed against these books, he remained nonplussed, for the books in the case were phonies, cheap old books picked up for pennies on the market. They were lightning rods designed to keep his good books from destruction.[13]

Dr. Johnson: Book-Slob Extraordinaire

Dr. Samuel Johnson, the incomparable writer and lexicographer—sagacious, eclectic, encyclopedic, eristic, learned, and wise—is worth every encomium we can heap on his glorious name. His feats of literary prodigiousness are without peer:

* * *

When he was still in petticoats his mother one morning gave him the Common Book of Prayer, pointed to the collect of the day, and said, "Sam, you must get this by heart." Then she walked up the stairs. Before she reached the top, she heard Sam following. "What's the matter?" she asked. "I can say it," he replied, and recited the collect.[1]

During his school career, he was never corrected by a teacher, apart from disciplinary problems. Because he was liberal with his assistance to his fellow students, three of them showed their reverence by bearing him to school in a reclining position on their backs.[2]

As for his writing method, he was fast and efficient under deadline pressure. He wrote forty-eight printed pages in one sitting once, although it took him all night.[3] He composed seventy lines of poetry in one day and didn't write a single line down until he had finished it in his head.[4] His essays for the *Idler* or the *Rambler* were dashed off with the rapidity of a casual letter, stuffed into an envelope and stuck in the mail.[5] Nearly all his *Rambler* essays were written just prior to press time—he sent the first part in and wrote the remainder while the first part was printing.[6]

* * *

No wonder nobody (except his mother) ever calls him Sam or Sammy or Samuel or even Johnson. It seems whenever his name comes up in literate converse, he is always referred to with the simple appellation Dr. Johnson.

Well, Dr. Johnson may have been one of a kind intellectual-like-wise (as Al Haig would say), but when it came to caring for his own volumes, he was a book slob nonpareil. His biographer, James Boswell, entered his library once, contained in two garrets over his chambers, and found "a number of good books, but very dusty and in great confusion."[7] Manuscript leaves in Johnson's handwriting littered the floor. Augustine Birrell noted that to put his books in order, the doctor donned huge, thick gloves like hedgers use, and then "clutching his folios and octavos, he banged and buffeted them together until he was enveloped in a cloud of dust."[8] After which he replaced them on the shelves, allowing the dust to resettle undisturbed.

And his manner of reading would send most of us into fits of frothed barking. Some of his closest friends refused to lend him books because they were horrified of his book habits.[9] He once commended a poet on his way of marking pages: When any passage the poet was reading pleased him, the poet folded down the leaf, which Johnson approved of. So many leaves had the poet folded down that many of his books would not even close.[10]

CHAPTER THIRTEEN

Lending

How hard, when those who do not wish
To lend, that's lose, their books,
Are snared by anglers—folks that fish
With literary hooks;

Who call and take some favourite tome,
But never read it through,—
They thus complete their set at home,
By making one at you.

Behold the bookshelf of a dunce
Who borrows—never lends;
Yon work, in twenty volumes once
Belonged to twenty friends.[1]

THERE ARE TWO TYPES OF BIBLIOHOLICS in this world: those who lend books and those who don't. Our heart commends those altruistic types who treat every tome as the property of the community. We extol their generosity and compassion and trust in the goodness of mankind.

But we excoriate their naiveté. For the cold truth is: Books lent are seldom returned.

An English writer tells the story of one bookophile, the owner of a country house, who, while showing his exemplary library to a visitor, was asked, "Do you ever lend books?" The Brahmin answered, "No, only fools lend books," after which he swept his arm across a large section of his library and added, "All those books once belonged to fools."[2]

As Holbrook Jackson so aptly put it, "A fool and his books are soon parted."[3] For with the generosity of meeting another reader's needs, with the effusive outpouring of our lifeblood to sustain another's interest, the fact is, we *will* get burned. Lending a book is tantamount to saying "adios" to it.

It is convenient for us, when we get burned, to impute to those who rip us off a pandemic, evil-spirited malevolent motive, to say, "That cheap scum is trying to rip off my books!" But that's being far too harsh on the borrower, and on ourselves. Consult your own shelves. Is there another's book (or books) ranged with your own? Most probably.

At some time in your book life, you were probably lent a book. You probably carried it home and set it apart from your own, pining to get to it. But things came up; other reads—more pressing, more enticing—availed themselves, and in the intervening days—and the intervening purchases—that borrowed tome was probably inexplicably mixed with the others. It was placed on your stacks and was incorpo-rated within your own thousands, and before long you most likely came to think of it as your own.

Biblioholics are continually visiting friends' libraries and, espying a tome of some familiarity on their shelves, pull it out and discover *their* name on the front endpaper. The habitual, ingenuous response from the unmasked friend is, "Oh, is that your book? I forgot." And we cock our heads and look at the borrower like he or she had just offered us a biblical defense of transvestitism. But think of it for a moment: Isn't that usually how it happens?

This, of course, in no way gainsays the evil intent of the true biblioklept. These are legion, a sordid breed, willing to enter into any form of deception to take unlawful possession of another's books. The stories of bibliokleptomania from the early days are troubling. One eighteenth-century papal nuncio named Passionei regularly emerged from the libraries of foreign abbeys "looking like a stuffed sausage for all the volumes concealed beneath his flowing cardinal's robes." Another of the prelate's tactics was to feign important research duties, lock himself in a library, and toss rare volumes out the window to a waiting myrmidon on the ground.[4] Other duplicitous officials stole manuscripts from provincial libraries, often taking the trouble to substitute sham volumes bound like the originals to cover up the deed.[5]

The lesson here is that despite our most sedulous precautions, if somebody wants to rip our books off, he or she will—our astute and studied eye notwithstanding.

The ultimate solution to getting borrowed books back is, of course, never to lend them in the first place. Establish a personal, ironclad credo never ever to lend a book and then don't back down from it no matter who, what, where, when, or why. But we are not automatons; we are human and we have *feelings*. And when some dewy-eyed picture of importunity fawns unremittingly over one of our books, hanging on our arms and pleading for us to lend it to him or her, we have to possess hearts made of tank armor to say no. We lend the book. Obviously, it's insane, but we do it anyhow.

The penultimate solution is damage control, that is, employing every means at our disposal to encourage the borrowed volume's return. These tactics number six:

* * *

1. Chain the books to your shelves. This is a time-honored deterrent to theft and has worked marvelously in times past, but requires some expense and can prove inconvenient.

2. Enter into draconian and proscriptive agreements with the borrower to ensure the tome's return. Richard de Bury lent books under the proviso that a "pledge" of equal or greater value than the borrowed book be deposited with him as collateral.[6] Appropriate "pledges" in our age may be the borrower's car, house, or children.

3. Writing your name in the book. This seems the most obvious safeguard, but there are esthetic considerations to deal with. Some biblioholics are so conscious of condition that they refuse to sully their tomes with any inscription whatsoever. Others write their names about a hundred times in various places in the book and then take a magic marker to the foreedge, the theory being that anybody can rip out a few of the pages, but nobody will rip out *all* of them. I had a high school teacher whose name, "Ackmann," writ large in ink, covered the foreedge of every one of his books. He always got them back. No doubt, the fact that he could turn back an Exocet missile with his gaze may have had something to do with it. Nonetheless, it worked.

Lending

Of course, the length to which one will go to identify the book as one's own is the crucial factor. What aesthetic price will you pay? Reports of bookhounds, exceedingly anxious for the return of a given book, who have written their names large and lusty on the title page just beneath some scrawl that was later identified as the signature of Teddy Roosevelt or Andrew Jackson, are troubling.

4. More subtle but no less effective is the practice of marking one's ownership of a given volume with a secret code known only to the owner. One option is emulating the public library, stamping one's name with garish rubber stamps at various spots in the book. Much better are the stamps that the goons at the door of a dance club stick on our right hands immediately after we pay the cover, which can be seen under special blue lights. And these should be stamped only at preordained places, like in the lower left corner of all pages that are multiples of thirty-seven, for example.

5. More classy by far is the bookplate. Many biblioholics go in for frilly stickers, garland encircled, with curlicues and arabesques wreathed all around the big block letters that say "Ex libris," under which they print their names. They think it looks like something from the personal bookshelf of, say, Charlemagne or Henry VIII, when in reality it more closely resembles something on a letter from the Westinghouse Sweepstakes.

You see this sort of thing all the time. On the title page of some book will stand a heraldic bookplate with spears and swords and coats of arms and laurel wreaths and all sorts of botanical symbols snaking serpentine around a huge open space which is filled, in an infantile scrawl, with something like "From the estate of Homer Fenwick Bolingbrooke, Esq." And later you discover that Homer Fenwick Bolingbrooke, Esq. is some eight-year-old kid who simply likes to write his name a lot.

Others go in for mottoes, usually written in Latin, which they think, if adhered to, will change the world. Others still take the symbolic approach, bestowing on their bookplates drawings illustrative of the author's predilections: drawings of a white suit for Tom Wolfe's books, boxing gloves for Norman Mailer's, bottles of bourbon for Faulkner's, a pair of glasses for Joyce's, or a joint for Kesey's, under which they scribble their names. All of this is well and good. It adds an intimate touch. And it infuses the volume with a little panache. But does it get the book back?

If biblioholics are going to make bookplates work, they must give them some teeth. Forget the frills and curlicues, forget the treacly words of wisdom. If you want that borrowed book back, you must get serious about what you write on your bookplates.

Writing "The one who steals this book will go directly to hell" would probably have made a valid point two hundred years ago when people still believed in hell. In fact, threats of comminatory justice are almost a tradition with certain bibliophiles. Pope Sixtus IV threatened anyone who failed to return a book from the Vatican Library within forty days with immediate excommunication.[7] But ours is an irreligious age. Threaten people with excommunication these days and they win elections.

Lending

We cannot rely on threats of spiritual unpleasantness. No, we must get physical. Consider the following verse, written above a line drawing of a gallows on the flyleaf of a book:

My Master's name above you se,
Take heede therefore you steale not mee;
For if you doe, without delay
Your necke . . . for me shall pay.
Looke doune below and you shall see
The picture of the gallowstree;
Take heede therefore of thys in time,
Lest on this tree you highly clime![8]

However, individualized anathemas, peculiar to the book in question, would probably be most effective. This requires a little imagination, but when the result is getting your borrowed book back, a little creativity is a small price to pay. What follows are some samples:

In Joyce's *Finnegans Wake:* "If you steal this book, may your mind be as jumbled and disjointed as this narrative."

In Charlotte Brontë's *Jane Eyre:* "If you steal this book, may all your in-laws be like Bertha Mason."

In Hemingway's *For Whom the Bell Tolls:* "If you steal this book, the earth will never move for you (wink, wink; nudge, nudge)."

In Fitzgerald's *Great Gatsby*: "I've got my eye on you."

In any Stephen King book: "If you steal this book, may your every dog be Cujo, your every car Christine, and your every child some whacked-out psycho who can start fires with her mind."

In any James Michener book: "He who steals this book shall be sentenced to read it twice."

6. As a last resort, we can take our cue from the public libraries of times past and institute our own personal "Conscience Week,"[9] wherein all books borrowed and not returned can be given back anonymously, without fear of retribution or condemnatory glances.

   For there comes a time in the life of every borrowed book that it becomes, in effect, too overdue to return. This is certainly true of library books—at some point the borrower says, "I can't return this book. It's sixteen years overdue!" And it is equally true of those we borrow from friends. The pain and embarrassment of shuffling up to a friend with a book, say, twelve years after borrowing it, is too much for even the most honest of us to shoulder. It is much easier merely to hope the lender has forgotten about it.

The Final Act

THE COMES A TIME in all of our lives—and a sad time it will be, too—when the treasures that have so often given us happiness and meaning will meet their end—with us, anyhow. The awful truth is, someday we are going to have to bid adieu to our beloved tomes. To do so voluntarily, of course, is best, and optimally this will come in some magnanimous act of largess performed from our deathbeds when we're about ninety-five years of age.

But sometimes it comes sooner. We actually have to sell them to keep alive. We can deny ourselves the necessities of life for only so long. Eventually, biological need forces us to do something, and that something is the inexorable decision to sell our books.

The act of letting go is arguably the most traumatic event of our book lives. And whether the treasure trove is dispersed to the Bodleian or to Merle and Maggie's Used Book Emporium, our bookish ways often go down, not in the alpenglow of eleemosynary munificence, but in the flames of agony.

Consider the case of Archdeacon Meadow, an early-era bookaholic who had accumulated such a store of books that necessity prompted him to conduct an auction. This is the same Archdeacon Meadow who, when summoned to the House of Commons to be examined by a committee, abruptly disappeared, only to return home some time later "followed by a waggon containing 372 copies of rare editions of the Bible"; the same Archdeacon Meadow who, when defeated at auction for a particular book once, allayed his grief by saying, "Well, so be it—but I daresay I have ten or twelve copies at home." Archdeacon Meadow was deep in the throes of the disease.

And the pain of seeing his own volumes dispersed at sale drove him to the depths of anguish. Squirming as the gavel pounded, growing ever more distraught with each of the auctioneer's peremptory swings, he could take it no longer and left the room, returning in the guise of a "military gentleman" to buy back his own books.[1]

CHAPTER FOURTEEN

The Cure

To be mad and know it

is half way to sanity.[1]

WELL, YOU'VE TRAVERSED THIRTEEN CHAPTERS of discussion on the virulent and debilitating aspects of this disease, you have delineated its deracinating ways, and now you're probably ready to bask in the good news of a cure and get on with life, right?

Well, not to put too fine a point on it, but *wrong*. Because the operative rule for this disease is: Biblioholic, heal thyself.

Nobody has found a cure for this rampant and emasculating illness. The experts have been batting the issue back and forth for centuries, positing this cure and that remedy, endorsing all sorts of rehabilitative enterprises, some of them more than a tad silly, and still nothing. Biblioholics of today are as enmired and entrammelled by their disease as were their counterparts two centuries ago.

However, there exist some methods that biblioholics seeking to be healed would do well to consider. These number five:

TOTAL ABSTINENCE

This is by far the most heinous and antiquated of all treatment methods, as most biblioholics go stark-raving mad just thinking about giving up their beloved books. And with good reason. Think of yourself for a moment; consider a life without them—consider even a day without them. It is enough to send one into Howard Hughesian reclusion—toilet paper, long fingernails and all.

And yet this totally woeful remedy is one increasingly pushed onto out-of-control biblioholics. In pious tones, counselors pull us into the confessional, listen gravely as we catalog our many excesses, forgive us our trespasses, and admonish us to go and sin no more. And they think that's going to cut it.

Just think, for a moment, what total abstinence from books would mean. Wrenched away from your bookish milieu and placed in a hostile, sterile, nonbook, nonreading environment. Walking into your home and finding absolutely no books anywhere. Slipping between the sheets at night and having no books by your bed. Reclining in your favorite reading chair with nothing to lay in your lap, nothing to hold in your hands, nothing to do with your eyes. Why, you'd have to watch television!

And what's more, the withdrawal would be absolutely brutal. What would it be like? you ask. How violent and forcefully would the heebie-jeebies hit us, were we to divorce ourselves absolutely from books? How bad would it be? Well, suffice it to say, it would not be pretty, as anyone who has ever gone through a period of total abstinence can attest to, and it would manifest itself, within a day's time, in the following behaviors:

Biblioholism: The Literary Addiction

* * *

1. An unwillingness to sit down, and a total avoidance of the favorite chair. Sitting carries with it many associations for many people, but to biblioholics sitting relates to one thing only: reading. Biblioholics sit at the breakfast table and read; they sit in the living room and read; they sit in the study and read; they sit at their desk and read. And when they sit, they are suffused with eager longing for the pleasure they anticipate, but now that they are off books entirely, all such attendant pleasures are gone. Look for little sitting during abstinence—the pain of association is too great.

2. An energetic ambition to do things with their hands, like weeding gardens, reshingling roofs, polishing cars, mowing the grass, and a hundred other chores that were anathematized during their bookish days. Biblioholics' hands are accustomed to holding books; the fingers are used primarily for turning pages. Once they swear off books, the biblioholic's hands have nothing to do. They're just weird things at the ends of their arms. So they put them to other uses. Some nonbiblioholic codependents may jump to the conclusion that this newfound ambition to use the hands would be good news for all involved; an often tragic disregard for property upkeep could be remedied with the repentant biblioholics now doing all the chores they neglected for the past, oh so many years. The house might get painted, the gutters might get cleaned out, the tires might get rotated, etcetera. But alas, there is a complication, and that is that biblioholics in withdrawal from books possess a universal vilification of

everything, everywhere. Biblioholics going off books cold turkey hate the world and everything in it. It has conspired to keep them from the one thing they love, and they are determined to make it pay.

* * *

The time has come to put the egregious total abstinence myth out to pasture. Taking people who are bookpeople down to their very fingertips, yanking them cold turkey from their bookish environments, and throwing them into some sterile, joyless life and expecting them for some reason to become happy, contented couch potatoes for the remainder of their lives is undiluted psychological pish-posh.

FIND SOMETHING ELSE TO LOVE

This cure is as old as the total abstinence cure and equally insidious, manifesting itself in concerned loved ones' pleas, like "Oh, if we could only get Pa to get off whiskey and start going to church," or "Now, if we could only get Junior to quit hanging around back of the barn smoking after school and get interested in the Latin Club, all our problems would be solved."

The problem in this reasoning, of course, is that Pa and Junior, unbeknownst to all concerned, would then probably become addicted to religion and Latin, respectively. The fact is, things have changed considerably since the Mas of the world wanted to get the Pas off the hooch and the Juniors off the weed. Addicts have popped up everywhere, and not only to hooch and angel dust and coffin nails. Now it's shopping, religion, fitness, rage, chocolate, sex, work, driving fast, pizza, and who knows what else. In fact, we are all addicts, or codependents, or in some way affected by someone with one of these horrendous diseases, such as shopaholism, workaholism, chocoholism, rushaholism, rageaholism, and on and on. It has been claimed by "wellness" industry spokesmen that 96 percent of all Americans suffer from codependency of some sort or another.[2] That's pert' near all of us, folks.

So, what does that mean for today's biblioholic? It means that if it's not going to be books, it's going to be something else, and as biblioholism is a disease drawing the most intellectual of people into its orbit, this new addiction is not likely to be something reasonably accessible like hubcaps, beer cans, or bullfighters on velvet. No, it's going to be van Gogh originals or eggshell porcelain or Mycenean goblets or something extravagantly pricey like that. This is one cure that is worse than the disease itself.

MARRIAGE

This is the tactic of only the most desperate biblioholic. For throughout history nothing has afflicted the bookperson's life like the nonbiblioholic spouse. These spouses can be loving, affectionate, loyal helpmeets who hang on their loved one's arms, shower him or her with kisses, and claim a love so enormous that neither sickness nor poverty, etc., etc., would ever take them from their beloved's side. But let this beloved be out buying books or be caught trying to spirit some of those illicitly purchased books into the house, or even engaged in untoward reading, and these heretofore zealously devoted spouses transmogrify into a cross between Genghis Khan and Freddy Krueger.

Think, for example, of the plight of one Judge Methuen, whose wife, when she observed him in his library with a volume of Pliny in his lap—gasp!—*two afternoons in a row*, locked the tome in the pantry.[3] Or poet F. Fertiault, who put his anguish to rhyme in "A Domestic Event":

> *Back from a tedious holiday*
> > *He comes, and—Duty first—he looks*
> > *Around for his familiar books;*
> *But all the room's in disarray!*
> *He searches, what's the matter, eh?*
> > *He hunts in most unheard of nooks.*
> > *"Were robbers here, or were they cooks,*
> *Who seized, who stole my Books away?*
> *Not one! What wind has blown about,*
> *What tempest can have tossed them out,*
> > *And cleared the shelves that used to hold them?"*
> *No cook, no thief, no tempest came,*
> *His lady wife 'tis she's to blame,*
> > *Who carted off the Books—and sold them![4]*

A rational, single, nonmasochistic biblioholic should think about marriage to a nonbiblioholic in much the same way as he or she thinks about gastrointestinal probes.

But still, there is no foretelling the ends to which desperation will push us, and, in at least one case, the marital bond proved powerful enough to defeat the disease. One latter-stage biblioholic named Christopherson slipped off the edge of sanity, voraciously haunting bookstalls, buying without compunction, and even when he had been reduced to poverty, continued his arrant ways, living on sixpence a day and accumulating more and more books. He sent his wife out to work for him, to provide more money with which to sate his desires, and while she did so joyfully, after a short time her health failed. Doctors prescribed life in the country as the elixir, and a relative even offered a cottage, free of rent, for the couple to use during rehabilitation, with one small proviso: the man could not bring his books along. Not surprisingly, the bookaholic refused to go. His wife's health grew worse, and only at the point of death did Christopherson relent. He sold most of his books, the couple moved to the country, and the wife's health was restored.[5]

But in cases like these, it can go either way. Some biblioholics will respond to the indulgent spouse; some won't. A person who will forego even food for books cannot be expected to give up a lifelong love for the mere companionship of a loved one.

BOOKWORMS

However, all the aforementioned cures attack only one part of the problem of biblioholism: the demand side. We have learned through our country's war on drugs that there exists another, equally powerful element of addiction: the supply side. So, you're probably thinking, now what? Battalions of marines posted in front of all the bookstores in the country? Battleships in the East River? The seriousness of the problem precludes all such foolish remedies. We offer an honest and ingenuous antidote intended to bring this vile and sweeping scourge under control: bookworms.

Bookworms have forever been a pox on the biblioholic's house. Since the invention of books, the malignant insect has found it prudent to feed on pulp, leather, and even bindings. And they are voracious, destroying *in toto* entire volumes, entire sets, entire libraries. In one disputed case, one bookworm is said to have burrowed a single tiny hole widthwise through a set of twenty-seven books.[6]

Given the advances in genetics in recent years, those seeking a cure for biblioholism must be enheartened. Indeed, special book-eating animals are not an altogether new concept. Eugene Field writes of a Dr. O'Rell, who invented a lymph which, when injected into Field's sister's cat, prompted the feline to enter Field's library—a place to which the cat had never before ventured—and ravage a copy of Rabelais.[7]

Genetic engineering presents some rather ominous possibilities for the book world as a whole, however. While, certainly, science could use it to moral ends—for example, codependents could unleash a cigar box full of them in the biblioholic's den and be codependents no more by morning—put into the wrong hands, this scientific ability could turn the book world upside down. Bookworms could be developed that hunger only for a certain sort of book, say, history, biography, or even literature. Bookworms could be programmed to eat only one author, or all authors but one. Collectomaniacs could hire crop dusters to fly over rivals' houses. The entire book world, or any given aspect of it, could be put under the finger of anyone who happened to be at the vanguard of scientific inquiry.

But, not to worry, scientific advances of such magnitude are some years down the pike. The question for us today is: If abstinence poses more problems than it solves, if marriage cannot be relied on to divert the book-lust to spouse-lust, and if genetically engineered bookworms are still in the R & D phase, what can be done now? Reason doesn't work, nagging doesn't work, anger doesn't work—we know all too well what doesn't work. Now, we get to crunch time. The big question is: What does? How are we, troubled by excess yet powerless to do anything about it, going to get healed?

BUY TILL IT HURTS

We have laid out this threat; we have outlined its destructive ways; we have consumed many words detailing the horror and abject deprivation that awaits those who allow their desire for books to romp unreined. We've heard all the warnings and we know of all the dangers, yet there we are, faithful and profligate, pulling books from the shelves of our favorite bookstore and fleeing home in maniacal joy.

Why do we do it? Are we moved by some woo-woo force that controls our being? Is the devil behind it all? Are we stupid? Or what?

First, the facts. Fact number one is, many of us don't want to be healed. We are in no way ready to countenance even the thought of arresting our behavior. We are adamant in our love for books and resolved to follow our addiction to whatever dreadful end awaits us, be it penury, obscurity, delusions of grandeur, or whatever.

And fact number two is, nothing works unless we want to be cured. From the stinking miasma called addiction, from the hellhole of penury and abject deprivation, must come the cry, tortured and importunate, for help.

It's a catch-22. We need to scrape our chin in the gutters of addiction before the desire for healing can lift our soul. And in order to hit that bottom we have to buy until it hurts, until every dollar forked over for a book brings with it concomitant pain and guilt. We can't be cured until we want help; we can't want help until we hit bottom; and we can't hit bottom until we become absolute book fools and buy until it causes us so much pain we will want help.

What does it all mean? Only this: don't worry, be happy. Buy books—lots and lots of them. Until it hurts so bad you don't want to buy again.

The Cure

Sure, it might be true that some of us will never reach that point. It might stand that lifetimes of buying and reading can be consumed without even the minutest regret; that poverty-stricken as the low-bottom biblioholic is, he or she is still a heckuva lot happier than a Trump who lives in many-splendored opulence without books.

But what can we do? How else can we ever get healed?

The disease must run its course. Only in total defeat is there victory. Only from the bottom can we see the top. Once we get there, we can turn it around.

But, as they say, getting there is half the fun. In the meantime, happy booking!

Afterword

YOU MAY KNOW IT OR YOU MAY NOT, but a new day has dawned for book lovers the world round, and especially for we who sometimes—okay, what sometimes? a lot of the time—go a little overboard in our love of books.

And no, I speak not of the ever-attenuating list of books available to us, of the emphasis publishers and bookstores place on best-sellers, thus limiting their offerings—and our selections. Nor do I speak of the decline of the independent bookstore, the fact that there are fewer and fewer of these sanctuaries of knowledge and wisdom and exploration, where we can kick around in ill-lit corners and find the sorts of volumes that had somehow slipped undetected past Hollywood moguls, where, who knows, we might even confront a Wilkie Collins or a George Meredith or a Wyndham Lewis or even *Sketches by Boz* staring out at us in all their now-forgotten glory; a little overlooked niche where we can get away from film tie-ins and *Dummies* Guides and *Chicken Soup* books and Venus and Mars books and OJ books and Princess Di books and Jackie O books and Martha Stewart books and JonBenet books and Michael Jordan books and Clinton impeachment books and even—best-case scenario here—*Tuesdays with Morrie*. I'm not talking about that. I'm not even talking about how coffee shops frequently have bookstores attached to them these days, and how the help in those coffee shops know way more about coffee than the help in the bookstores know about books.

No, this is bigger than that. It's bigger than Harry Potter. Indeed, it's bigger than Oprah—and even her book club.

Afterword

And it isn't even an "it," technically speaking. It is something that is not something—a non-it. It weighs nothing; it takes no space; it cannot be stacked on a shelf or carried home in a sack or thrown at the cat or set beneath the legless corner of a couch. It does not have covers; it does not have dust jackets; it does not have ink, nor paper, nor glue, nor bindings. You can't look at it; you can't admire it or smell it or feel it or stroke its fine lineaments.

This "it" is but subatomic particles, electrons, whizzing through wires and eventually appearing on a little lighted screen you hold in your hand. When you turn off the screen, it goes away, not to the shelf on your wall or the stack beside your bed or the "architectural pile" on your floor, but to nowhere. It does not exist; it occupies no corporeal coordinates on the time-space continuum.

But enough about its it-ness—or lack thereof. It's here, it's real, it's scary, and we are going to have to deal with it.

I am speaking of the electronic book, the E-book.

You may derive from my tone that I am something of a Luddite, the sort who took his first look at a cell phone and said, "Like that'll ever fly. Like people want to be that available." I recognize this and do not shy away from its implications. In fact, I've always stood tall in proud defiance of the march of science and technology across our society.

And it is entirely possible that, in the area of books, you empathize with my innate Luddism. We book lovers have built our entire lives around these things, these objects, called books. We buy them, we stack them, we pull them down from our stacks, we riffle through their pages, we smell them, we read them (or at least some of them), and then we restack them. We do this many, many times. And then the next day, we repeat the process. It is a *very* pleasurable and meaningful series of events for us.

197

Biblioholism: The Literary Addiction

We are the sorts of people who enjoy characteristics of books like heft, who notice how thick the paper is, who have actually formed firm opinions on font types, who become aroused when we see larger-than-usual dust jacket flaps. Our idea of a profound experience is sitting in a room gazing longingly at our "lovelies" as they stand at attention in regal array.

We still rule the book world, true. E-book aficionados are still kind of . . . well, out there, if you catch my meaning, gadgeteer types who computerize their interior lighting and speak to their kitchen appliances—"Cuisinart on! Toaster on!" Most of them probably wear their baseball caps backward and spend a lot of time attempting to extricate Zelda from the malevolent grasp of the evil Ganondorf. But as time goes on, they will grow up and assume important positions in the boardrooms of commerce and the cubicles of government—just as we boomers did—and, one must assume, will comport themselves with equal gravity and respect for tradition.

As for us print-and-paper book hounds, alas, we will eventually die. And the ranks of future book lovers coming behind us, the ones who will sustain our proud tradition, may not share our nongeek outlook on life. Whipping out their Palm Pilots wherever they happen to be and coursing through Stephen King's latest will be the norm in this brave new book world. Accessing books at any time and place will be commonplace with future readers. The rabid among them may even live what to us is now unthinkable—totally paperless lives.

In case you haven't heard, the utopia that awaits us is configured thusly: All books ever printed will be downloaded into databases classified by categories and made available in every known language. Sitting at your computer, you browse around these databases and choose a book you want to buy. That book is then downloaded onto your computer for you to read from the comfort of your five-wheeler; or it is dispatched to a kiosk somewhere (an E-Kinko's or a glorified E-ATM machine), where an individual copy of your book is printed out and bound; or it is downloaded from your computer onto a hand-held digitized reading device, which you can carry around in your jeans pocket like you did Camus or Hesse during college. As many as ten complete works will be available for the "end content user" (formerly called reader) from these little glowing machines.

These "books" (forgive the scare quotes) will be exceedingly cheap, for the many middlemen now feeding off the publishing process will be obviated. Publishers won't have to worry about paper costs, plates and printing costs, storage and shipping costs, the cost of taking returned volumes, the cost of detailed sales strategies, costs for cover art and dust jackets; they won't have to hire people to lobby for eye-level outward-facing shelf positions; nor must they construct cardboard sixteen-volume display cases for newly minted volumes. Why not? Because they are no longer selling books as we understand them. Colliding electrons, it seems, are intensely labor friendly.

That's what the future looks like. The question is: Where do we biblioholics fit in?

Once we get over the fact that we will be book lovers living in a world with very few corporeal, palpable objects called books—therapy, no doubt, will be available—it might not be so bad. It'll be *different*, no question about it. But that's how it is in an ever-changing world. The monks of the Middle Ages probably didn't like it one little bit when this guy Gutenberg arrived on the scene and swept away their inkpots and quills. But they got over it—indeed, their scions became our forebears in book love.

And, after a brief adjustment period, so will we. The way I see it, we will have to change three basic areas of our lives: browsing and conversing, buying and storing, and reading. While it is true that these three areas are of reasonable importance to our current mode of living—indeed, we have no sentient lives whatsoever without them— alas, fellow biblioholics, the future is not going to stop just for us. We'll just have to work through that.

Accompany me as we peer courageously into this brave new world.

BROWSING AND CONVERSING

The way it used to work long, long ago—perhaps as early as 1995— was, if we were smitten by a sudden hankering to browse a bookstore or converse with others about our beloved treasures, we were pretty much at the mercy of the powers that be. Regarding the former, we could only browse when a bookstore allowed us to—usually between, say, 10 A.M. and 10 P.M.—and what's more, we had to haul our tails down to that bookstore before we could traipse the holy aisles and commune with the bountiful stacks. As for book converse, it was pretty barren in the olden, pre-E–everything times. I used to go hours—sometimes *days*—before I happened across a kindred spirit who wanted to discuss the early novels of Evelyn Waugh, one of my favorite topics. (Who am I kidding? I haven't found a dialogue partner on this subject for *fifty-one years*.)

The Internet has changed all that. Now, when I bolt upright in the middle of the night thinking, "I'd like to read some reviews of Spenser's *Faerie Queene*"—it has to be all that ice cream I eat before I go to bed— I can simply power up the Pentium and cruise about until I find them. Or if at halftime of the Broncos game I get this deep desire to colloquize with some fellow traveler on Dryden's *Absalom and Achitophel,* again I can repair to cyberspace and dispatch my cry of need.

Afterword

By availing myself of Amazon.com or bn.com (Barnes and Noble's website) and countless websites devoted to literary discussion, I can rub the prints off my fingers before satiating my browsing and conversing needs. The links from one book lead to another; those links to another; those to more and more and more and . . . well, you can sample more books in a few hours than Dickens has characters. And you don't even have to *walk*. For example, I logged on to Michael Crichton's latest, *Timeline,* read all the reviews, was directed by the friendly Amazon people—"Customers who bought this book also bought:"—to Scott Turow, James Patterson, and Nelson Demille. Soon I was tossing Robert Ludlums and Michael Connellys and Ed McBains and forty-three other writers I had never heard of into my cyber-shopping cart as quickly as my mouse finger would allow. And when, soon thereafter—we biblio-holics are nothing if not eclectic—I found myself bidding on a signed first edition of *Little Women* and an unsigned first of *For Whom the Bell Tolls,* I decided to call it a spree and get out. Only my lack of a credit card—some of us are also poor, not to mention a little behind the times—prevented me from completing the Mother of All Book Browses.

As for book conversation, again one is limited only by one's stamina. In fact, a plebeian bookaholic with no literary bona fides whatever except way too many stacks of books around his place can transcend his humble status and become a genuine book critic—perhaps even one of Amazon's elite "Top 500" or "Top 50" or "Top 10" reviewers. What I have learned from this experience is that, however idiotic my opinions, others will take them *seriously*. What I have also learned is that they don't like them very much, as reflected in words like "1 of 342 readers found this review helpful."

As mentioned above, all that is available right now compliments of the Internet. But there is certainly room for improvement, upgrades in service and accessibility that will doubtless accompany E-books' rise to dominance. For, as of now, the time span between the browse and the purchase remains exceedingly inconvenient. You can browse at 2 A.M., certainly. You can even buy the book you just perused at 2 A.M. And you can add hundreds of others to your wish list, should you so desire. But the way things currently stand, those books will not descend into your eager hands until at least *two days* thereafter. They are, after all, still print-and-paper books, tangible objects that must be pulled off warehouse shelves, shrink-wrapped, thrown onto an airplane and then a truck, and walked up to your door.

E-books eliminate that painful—and needless—delay. Once you buy an E-book, that thing is in your possession immediately. And it is to the purchase and storing of these "volumes" that we now turn.

BUYING AND STORING

Let's say you're driving down the freeway listening to talk radio. Let's also say the guest on afternoon-drive is Joyce Carol Oates. Let's further say you are intrigued by the interview and suddenly get the urge to read Oates in great quantity. What will you do to sate your biblioholic yearnings?

Will you drop into a superstore and pop $80 on the four Oates titles available on the shelves, placing orders for seven others and waiting an eternity—*six weeks*—for them to arrive, at which time you must motor down to the same superstore and pony up another $80 to $120 for the privilege of lugging them home?

Or will you speed directly home and immediately download the entire Oates oeuvre onto your computer or handheld reading machine, paying maybe $20 for the lot, and if you desire actual paper-and-ink versions, feed some colliding electrons into a rudimentary printing device and watch it print and bind the Oates corpus right in front of your eyes? Technophobe though I be, I think I could get used to this second option.

The fact that every book ever printed will be as close to our eyes and hands as a few mouse clicks will radically alter life as we biblio-holics know it. For one thing, out-of-print books will cease to exist. Now, on the surface this does not seem entirely positive, for it also means no books will stop in that purgatory of the publishing world called remainderdom. And are not some of our most blissful times spent slumming through the bargain book shelves? Do not some of our most precious finds come from that final rest stop on a given tome's journey to the pulping machine? Well, yes and yes. But remember this: the reason no books will reach remainderdom is because no books will ever go out of print. And that's because publishers won't publish four million copies of a best-seller and then feed three million of them to the whirling steel blades a few months later. They'll publish only on demand—only so many as are ordered. And they won't even publish those per se—they'll send them to your computer.

This is very radical stuff. All the books we always wanted to read but could never find, as close as our mousepad; heck, all the books we ever wanted to read and could find, and even all the books we don't want to read but still wouldn't mind having around our house, being equally close—must I spell out what this means? The entire Library of Congress could conceivably be transferred to that little buzzing box in your workstation in the course of a day or so. I believe even the most technophobic among you will join me in a silent moment of thanks-giving for this turn of events.

Spending all Saturday traveling the used and antiquarian bookstore circuit looking for *Stanley and the Women* or *The Anti-Death*

League or other lesser-known Kingsley Amises will be but a chapter in our biblioholic past, for all of Kinsley Amis will be perpetually available. Those early Trollopes that you can never find—they'll be there as well, zipping around in the ether and awaiting a beckoning click. Same for the sixty or so Wodhouses that never make it to the bookstore shelves. Obscure novels that flashed for six weeks before our eyes and then disappeared—like William Faulkner's first novel, or Robert James Waller's *second*—will never get away again. This can only be seen as a revolutionary development.

I, for one, look forward to the day that I can see clearly again—for the day when these eye-high stacks of books that encircle my desk and occlude my view out my sliding doorway are gone, replaced with ankle-high stacks of CDs. I eagerly anticipate the day when I can transit the short distance from my desk to my bathroom without summoning up a Barry Sanders running style to avoid my myriad "architectural piles"; when I can open my Beefaroni cupboard unfearful that my stacks of Diane Mott Davidson and Jill Churchill—I stack creatively— will not send me crashing to the linoleum; when I can go to sleep untroubled by the off chance that my bedside towers will topple onto my head and send me the way of all flesh. What's more, for the first time in twelve years, I will be able to move.

But that could be the non-addict in me talking. Once E-books show their publishing might, it may not be so easy to shake a lifetime of obsession over these physical objects called books. You can't smell electrons, after all. Reading solely off computer screens or Palm Pilots may not silence the inner voices; not having our "beauties" arrayed about us may leave us perpetually disconsolate, for they are our refuge; their mere presence about us offers comfort; just having them around makes everything okay.

Afterword

Thus, I could see myself printing the books I download and relapsing to my biblioholic past, my view out my window obscured not by eye-high stacks of books but by head-high reams of *copy paper*. I'll still have four white walls in my bedroom and cement-to-rafters stacks of books in my garage. And I'll still have no furniture.

Besides which, book posing (biblionarcissism) is likely to disappear entirely in an E-book world. Lamentable though it be, all of us biblioholics suckle on occasion the faux prestige that redounds to us by slipping an important work under our arms and walking around. "I am a serious person," this action says. "As testimony to this fact, please observe that Sophocles' *Oedipus at Colonus* is firmly lodged beneath my arm as I stroll importantly about." E-books do not possess this same cache. Put a digital reading device under your arm, and you're not that dissimilar to the guy walking down the sidewalk talking too-loudly on his cell phone (although you are less obnoxious). As for the posing possibilities of the well-stocked show bookshelf, where eleven-volume histories of civilization vie for space with complete sets of, oh, Kant or Hume or Locke, this will also be precluded in an E-book world by the simple fact that E-books are *invisible* to the human eye.

And then there is a certain word that pops into technological conversation every now and again: *obsolescence*. Books as we know them are reasonably stable entities. When we close a book after an evening's read, the print on the pages does not whiz off to some cyber-warehouse, to be retrieved when we next decide to take it up again. Should we wait fifty years before we return to that book, we'll still be able to "access" it. Not so with E-books, however. Who knows how many generations of digital reading devices, each outmoding the last, will travel across our laps in the next ten years, much less fifty? Each one of those things is going to cost you three figures, my friends—

maybe twenty hardbacks' worth of books. And what, pray tell, are you going to do with the two thousand paper-and-ink books that will be made redundant by the two thousand identical E-books you buy? Put them in your attic next to the five hundred cassette tapes obviated by their identical five hundred compact disks?

E-books or no, we will probably never outgrow our need for traditional bookstores. But these stores, ironically, may change along with us, for with the convenience and savings proffered by E-books, superstores will suddenly become much less super. Bookstores in the E-future may transmogrify into the sorts of places we wish they were today—humble little streetside shops where the talk is cheap (and so is the coffee).

READING

There is certainly no mystery involved in reading a paper-and-ink book—it's a pretty perspicuous enterprise. You sit on the bus bench absorbed in some tech-thriller awaiting your morning conveyance, and people can take one look at you and say, "Yep. That fellow's reading a book." Nor is there, in these times, much mystique about computers; everybody has one, most people work on them, a lot of them even talk about them in their spare time. The world is fully aware of the computer's elastic capabilities. "So, you're reading a book on a computer? No big deal." But reading a book from a handheld digitized reading machine is quite the cryptic event.

For, truth be told, the casual observer has absolutely no idea what one poking around on a Palm Pilot is actually doing. He may be plowing through *Tristram Shandy* or *The Mill on the Floss,* true, but he might also be saying hi to the ladies at the Victoria's Secret website.

Unless you physically stick your head between his eyes and his reading device, you just don't know for sure.

It will be a few years before digital reading machines go mainstream, before those punching their styluses into the holes on a Rocket eBook are not thought of more as hopeless digerati than as bona fide book people, but when they do, I guarantee it will change the face of the one thing we have devoted our lives to: reading.

Having at our instant command at all times of every day or night every book ever printed will be a heck of a lot of fun. Consider the possibilities. You're at the communal coffee pot taking a break from your programming duties and schmoozing with your fellow cube-farm inmates, and the obnoxious office guy, a know-it-all type who is forever misusing the Queen's English, starts talking about the "enormity" of his current project, meaning he thinks it's really, really big. You have spoken to him before about his misappropriation of this term, but he has always dismissed your entreaties with disdain. This time, though, you're ready. You reach into your back jeans pocket for your Palm Pilot and wave it before his face. You say, "See this? This is the unabridged *Oxford English Dictionary*. Let's take a look at the etymology of enormity, shall we?"

It's kaffeeklatsch time at an academic symposium, and you and another pointy-head are laying it on very thick to a rep from the Ford Foundation who has announced he has $67,000 in grant money he wants to give away. You are standing in a circle, you three, with your styrofoam cups leaning against your chests, deep in argle-bargle about all things deconstructionistic. You make some brilliant point about *differance* or some such, and the rival egghead laughs out loud and says, "That is a ridiculous interpretation of Derrida." You feign shock and disgust before registering a look of surprise on your face. "Well, looky-here," you say, reaching into a pocket of your elbow-patched herringbone, "I just happen to have the entire Derrida corpus on me at the moment. Let's see what the 'boa-deconstructor,' as he has been called, has to say." And you whip out your Rocket eBook, punch up a work, scroll to the relevant page, read the quote verbatim (and get the grant).

You're seated in a charabanc seeing the sights of London. While your fellow pilgrims are restricted to but one or two guidebooks, which they haul about in their cumbersome paper-and-print form, you have, as close as a stylus poke, the germane Fodor's, Frommer's, Insight, Cadogan, Rick Steves', Time Out, Lonely Planet, Eyewitness, Let's Go, and Michelin Green guidebooks—all loaded onto your Palm Pilot prior to the trip. By the midpoint of the day's tour, you have so edified the group with your unlimited knowledge of the sights that the tour guide has hauled you to the front of the bus and presented you with the microphone. You become the hero of the bus, the object of constant adulation. You don't have to buy your own beer for two solid weeks.

Or, another travel vignette: You are taking your yearly winter holiday in the Caribbean, and plan on sitting for an entire week on a beach chair on the sands of Aruba. You will imbibe your share of umbrella drinks, certainly, but you'll also whisk through at least a dozen "beach" novels. Your record, set in 1998, is eighteen—two and a half a day. You had so many paperbacks in your suitcase that year you had to travel with one bathing suit and one pair of shoes. This year, because you have loaded twenty-four Mary Higgins Clarks and Dean Koonces and John Grishams and Carol Clarks and Nelson Demilles onto two handheld reading devices, you were able to arrive fully accou-tred, and even have room to return with that six-piece set of coconut-shell drinking cups you've always wanted.

Obviously, a world where all books are available at all times, acces-sible through a little device no larger than a portable calculator, will be very strange environs for we who have devoted our lives to palpable objects called books and have, at our fingertips, tons of paper and ink that testify to our obsession.

It will offer us abundant pleasure, certainly, but it will be a pretty odd place, a world where some of our habits will die a hard and miserable death. Take the matter of bookmarks, for example. Reading a volume from a Rocket eBook is tantamount to reading an ever-rejuvenating page—in short, a palimpsest. One turns no actual pages; one never progresses physically through a tome; and thus one cannot in any palpable sense enjoy the progress made in a given day of reading. This may seem a captious cavil, but charting the march of the bookmark from first page to last is one of the great joys I derive from the reading experience, and not always because I'm enjoying the tome in my hands. For example, if I ever decide to tackle *Buddenbrooks,* I will want to know, at every moment, exactly how many pages I have to slog through until I finish. A physical bookmark, a thick piece of paper (preferably acid-free), allows me that pleasure.

It is also currently impossible to identify salient passages from an E-book with, for example, a Magic Marker (oh, you certainly can, but for all practical purposes you can only mark one such passage per handheld reading machine). And because of the nature of technology—it is hegemonic; it makes you think about it even when you don't want to—losing oneself in a book, as was common with our beloved print-and-paper volumes, will be tantamount to impossible.

The E-book industry acknowledges this and is taking steps to eliminate these problems. For the E-book industry is nothing if not smart, and it realizes that what it is trying to improve upon is pretty good just the way it is. Let's face it, print-and-paper books are pretty convenient. They're easy to read, they're light, they're manageable, they're portable, their pretty cheap, they're accessible in a technology that won't soon be obsolescent, and they don't need batteries.

E-books, in turn, want to be everything print-and-paper books already *are*.

Maybe they will become that; maybe they won't. But looking on the bright side, whether E-books come to dominate the business, whether the world decides en masse that the unimprovable cannot be improved upon, or whether some hybrid of virtual books and real books eventually carries the day—the most likely outcome—we who love to read words artistically arranged in units called sentences, and who are bent on accumulating vast collections of these words and arraying them about our living quarters, we won't be changed all that much.

We will still read books. We will still buy books—probably too many. And we will still love them—probably too much.

That's what we do. We are biblioholics.

Endnotes

Chapter ONE

1. John Ferriar, "The Bibliomania," in *Ballads of Books,* ed. Andrew Lang (London and New York: Longmans, Green, and Co., 1888), 115.

Chapter TWO

1. Henry Ward Beecher, *Star Papers; or, Experiences of Art and Nature* (New York: J. C. Derby, 1855), 251–52.
2. Robert A. Wilson, *Modern Book Collecting* (New York: Alfred A. Knopf, 1980), 32.
3. Nicholas Parsons, *The Book of Literary Lists* (New York: Facts on File Publications, 1987), 55.
4. Samuel Pepys, *Diary*, ed. Henry B. Wheatley, vol. 7 (1893; reprint, London: George Bell and Sons, 1905; originally published 1825), 344.
5. Leigh Hunt, *The Autobiography of Leigh Hunt* (London: Humphrey Milford, Oxford University Press, 1928; originally published 1850), 25–26.
6. Apuleius, *The Apology and Florida of Apuleius of Madaura*, trans. H. E. Butler (1909; reprint, Westport, CT: Greenwood Press, 1970), 25.
7. Thomas Frognall Dibdin, *Bibliomania* (London: McCreery, 1811), 57.
8. Michel de Montaigne, "Of the Education of Children," in *The Essays of Michel de Montaigne*, trans. Charles Cotton; ed. W. Carew Hazlitt, vol. 1 (New York: A. L. Burt Co., 1892), 163.
9. George Gissing, *The Private Papers of Henry Ryecroft* (London: Constable and Co., 1903), 36–37.
10. Gustave Mouravit, as cited in Holbrook Jackson, *The Anatomy of Bibliomania*, rev. ed. (New York: Scribner's Sons, 1932), 676.
11. Charles and Mary Elton, *The Great Book-Collectors* (London: Kegan Paul, Trench, Trubner & Co., 1893), 99.
12. Percy Fitzgerald, *The Book Fancier* (London: Sampson, Low, Marston and Co., n.d.), 1.
13. Eugene Field, *The Love Affairs of a Bibliomaniac* (New York: Scribner's Sons, 1896), 98.

Biblioholism: Weakness or Disease?

1. Leslie Stephen, *Swift* (1882; reprint, London: Macmillan & Co., 1908), 3.
2. George Walter Prothero, as cited in Holbrook Jackson, *The Anatomy of Bibliomania*, rev. ed. (New York: Scribner's Sons, 1932), 252–53.
3. Edmund Gosse, *Father and Son: A Study in Two Temperaments* (London: William Heinemann, 1908), 21.
4. Frederic William Henry Myers, as cited in Jackson, *Anatomy of Bibliomania*, 255.

Chapter THREE

1. Spanish proverb, cited in *The International Thesaurus of Quotations*, comp. Rhoda Thomas Tripp (New York: Thomas Y. Crowell, Publishers, 1970), 268.

Chapter FIVE

1. Charles Nodier, indirect quotation in *Tales for Bibliophiles,* ed. and trans. Theodore W. Koch (1929; reprint, Freeport, NY: Books for Libraries Press, 1972), 154–55.
2. Koch, *Tales for Bibliophiles*, 23–25.
3. Jean de La Bruyère, as cited in Koch, *Tales for Bibliophiles,* 27.
4. Koch, *Tales for Bibliophiles*, 13.
5. Ibid., 24.
6. Seymour de Ricci, *English Collectors of Books & Manuscripts (1530–1930)* (Cambridge: University Press, 1930), 102.
7. Thomas Frognall Dibdin, *Reminiscences of a Literary Life*, vol. 1 (London: John Major, 1836), 436–37.

Chapter SIX

1. Joseph Addison, "Tom Folio," in *The Tatler*, 13 April 1710, as quoted in *Carrousel for Bibliophiles*, ed. William Targ (New York: Philip C. Duschnes, 1947), 151.
2. Dave Barry, *Dave Barry's Greatest Hits* (New York: Fawcett Columbine, 1988), 17.

Endnotes

3. Frederick Locker-Lampson, *My Confidences: An Autobiographical Sketch Addressed to My Descendants*, 2d ed. (London: Smith, Elder, & Co., 1896), 197.
4. Walter T. Spencer, *Forty Years in My Bookshop* (Boston and New York: Houghton Mifflin, 1923), 31.
5. John Hill Burton, *The Book-Hunter*, ed. J. Herbert Slater (London: George Routledge & Sons; New York: E. P. Dutton & Co., n.d.), 51.
6. Mark Twain, *The Innocents Abroad* (New York: Signet Classic New American Library, 1966; originally published 1869), 211–12.
7. A.S.W. Rosenbach, *Books and Bidders* (Boston: Little, Brown and Co., 1927), 39.
8. Philip S. Foner, *Mark Twain: Social Critic* (New York: International Publishers, 1958), 40–41.
9. Twain, *The Innocents Abroad*, 210.
10. Salvatore J. Iacone, *The Pleasures of Book Collecting* (New York: Harper & Row, Publishers, 1976), 54.

Chapter SEVEN

1. Publilius Syrus, cited in *The International Thesaurus of Quotations*, comp. Rhoda Thomas Tripp (New York: Thomas Y. Crowell, Publishers, 1970), 430.
2. Thomas de Quincey, *The Note Book of an English Opium-Eater* (Boston: James R. Osgood & Co., 1873), 252–53.
3. Eugene Field, *The Love Affairs of a Bibliomaniac* (New York: Scribner's Sons, 1896), 168–70.
4. Frederic Rowland Marvin, *The Excursions of a Book-Lover* (Boston: Sherman, French & Co., 1910), 10–11.
5. Frederick Locker-Lampson, *My Confidences: An Autobiographical Sketch Addressed to My Descendants*, 2d ed. (London: Smith, Elder, & Co., 1896), 197–99.
6. W. G. Clifford, "Books in Bottles," in *Bouillabaisse for Bibliophiles*, ed. William Targ (Metuchen, NJ: Scarecrow Reprint Corp., 1955), 158.
7. Thomas Jefferson Hogg, *The Life of Percy Bysshe Shelley* (London: George Routledge and Sons; New York: E. P. Dutton & Co., 1906), 62.
8. Francis Darwin, *The Life and Letters of Charles Darwin*, vol. 1 (London: J. Murray, 1888), 150–51.
9. James Taylor, as cited in Holbrook Jackson, *The Anatomy of Bibliomania*, rev. ed. (New York: Scribner's Sons, 1932), 537–38.
10. Marvin, *Excursions of a Book-Lover*, 10.

11. Nicholas Parsons, *The Book of Literary Lists* (New York: Facts on File Publications, 1987), 56.

Chapter EIGHT

1. Sebastian Brandt, "Ship of Fools," as quoted in Percy Fitzgerald, *The Book Fancier* (London: Sampson, Low, Marston & Co., n.d.), 3.
2. Holbrook Jackson, *The Anatomy of Bibliomania*, rev. ed. (New York: Scribner's Sons, 1932), 163.
3. Charles Caleb Colton, *Lacon, or, Many Things in Few Words; Addressed to Those Who Think*, rev. ed. (New York: W. Gowans, 1855; originally published 1820), 258.
4. Eugene Field, *The Love Affairs of a Bibliomaniac* (New York: Scribner's Sons, 1896), 34–35.
5. Joseph Epstein, *Plausible Prejudices* (New York: W. W. Norton & Co., 1985), 35. Used with permission.
6. Tad Tuleja, *The Catalog of Lost Books* (New York: Fawcett Columbine; published by Ballantine Books, a division of Random House, 1989), xiv–xv. Used with permission.
7. Anonymous, *The Returne from Pernassus* (London, 1606), as quoted in *Bouillabaisse for Bibliophiles*, ed. William Targ (Metuchen, NJ: Scarecrow Reprint Corp., 1955), 367.
8. Joseph Epstein, *Once More around the Block* (New York: W. W. Norton & Co., 1987), 95. Used with permission.
9. Epstein, *Plausible Prejudices*, 283–84.
10. William Waller, as quoted in Jackson, *Anatomy of Bibliomania*, 751.

Chapter NINE

1. Henry Ward Beecher, *Star Papers; or, Experiences of Art and Nature* (New York: J. C. Derby, 1855), 250.
2. Eugene Field, *The Love Affairs of a Bibliomaniac* (New York: Scribner's Sons, 1896), 135–36.
3. Ibid., 137.
4. Andrew Lang, *The Library* (London: Macmillan & Co., 1881), 31.
5. Holbrook Jackson, *The Anatomy of Bibliomania*, rev. ed. (New York: Scribner's Sons, 1932), 679.
6. Ibid., 596.
7. Ibid., 671.

8. Nicholas Parsons, *The Book of Literary Lists* (New York: Facts on File Publications, 1987), 116.

Getting Them into the House

1. Ben Abramson, "On Getting Books into the Home," in *Carrousel for Bibliophiles*, ed. William Targ (New York: Philip C. Duschnes, 1947), 75–76.
2. Ibid., 76–77.
3. Henry Ward Beecher, *Star Papers; or, Experiences of Art and Nature* (New York: J. C. Derby, 1855), 253–54.

Chapter TEN

1. Ben Jonson, "To My Bookseller," in *Ballads of Books*, ed. Andrew Lang (London: Longmans, Green and Co., 1888), 10.
2. Lewis Meyer, *The Customer Is Always* (Garden City, NY: Doubleday & Co., 1965), 87–88.
3. Edward Shils, "The Bookshop in America" in *The American Reading Public: What It Reads, Why It Reads*, ed. Roger H. Smith (New York: R. R. Bowker Co., 1962), 144.
4. Eugene Field, *The Love Affairs of a Bibliomaniac* (New York: Scribner's Sons, 1896), 122–23.
5. Ibid., 123.

Chapter ELEVEN

1. Logan Pearsall Smith, *All Trivia* (New York: Harcourt, Brace and Co., 1945), 177.
2. Pliny, *Letters*, trans. William Melmoth, rev. W.M.L. Hutchinson, vol. 2 (1915; reprint, Cambridge, MA: Harvard University Press; London: William Heinemann, 1952; originally published 1746), 153.
3. Joseph Spence, *Observations, Anecdotes, and Characters of Books and Men*, ed. James M. Osborn, vol. 1 (Oxford: Clarendon Press, 1966; originally published 1771), 178.
4. Philip Gilbert Hamerton, *The Intellectual Life* (Boston: Roberts Brothers, 1887), 192.
5. John Wesley, *The Journal of John Wesley*, ed. Nehemiah Curnock, rev. ed., vol. 5 (1914; reprint, London: The Epworth Press, 1938; originally published 1739), 360–61.

6. Holbrook Jackson, *The Anatomy of Bibliomania*, rev. ed. (New York: Scribner's Sons, 1932), 303.

7. Ibid., 298.

8. J. A. Symonds, as quoted in Jackson, *Anatomy of Bibliomania*, 325.

9. Jackson, *Anatomy of Bibliomania*, 325.

10. Malcolm K. Macmillan, as cited in Jackson, *Anatomy of Bibliomania*, 308.

11. The illustration by Aubrey Beardsley appears in Oscar Wilde, *Salome* (New York: Illustrated Editions Co., 1931; originally published 1892), 93.

12. Eugene Field, *The Love Affairs of a Bibliomaniac* (New York: Scribner's Sons, 1896), 31.

13. John Collings Squire, "Reading in Bed," in *Essays at Large* (Port Washington, NY: Kennikat Press, 1968; originally published 1922), 3.

14. Herbert A. Giles, *A Chinese Biographical Dictionary*, vol. 2 (London: B. Quaritch; Shanghai: Kelly & Walsh, 1898), 506.

15. Ibid., 688.

16. Jackson, *Anatomy of Bibliomania*, 290.

17. Ibid., 315.

18. Pliny, *Letters*, vol. 1, 203.

19. Archibald Philip Primrose Rosebery, *Miscellanies Literary & Historical*, vol. 2 (London: Hodder and Stoughton, 1921), 211–12.

20. Ronald J. Zboray, "Antebellum Reading and the Ironies of Technological Innovation," in *Reading in America*, ed. Cathy N. Davidson (Baltimore: Johns Hopkins University Press, 1989), 192.

21. Joseph Hall, as quoted in Jackson, *Anatomy of Bibliomania*, 309.

22. Charles Lamb, *The Essays of Elia* (New York: A. C. Armstrong & Son, 1888), 218.

23. Field, *Love Affairs of a Bibliomaniac*, 34.

24. Ibid., 32.

25. G. O. Trevelyan, *The Life and Letters of Lord Macaulay*, vol. 1 (New York: Harper & Brothers, 1904), 118.

26. Thomas Jefferson Hogg, *The Life of Percy Bysshe Shelley* (London: George Routledge and Sons; New York: E. P. Dutton & Co., 1906), 84.

27. Charles and Mary Elton, *The Great Book-Collectors* (London: Kegan Paul, Trench, Trubner & Co., 1893), 100.

Chapter TWELVE

1. The Old Librarian's Almanack by "Philobiblos" (Jared Bean) (New Haven, CT: 1773), as quoted in Slade Richard Gandert, *Protecting Your Collection*

(New York: The Haworth Press, 1982), ix. Used with permission.

2. Eugene Field, *The Love Affairs of a Bibliomaniac* (New York: Scribner's Sons, 1896), 235–36.

3. Edmund Gosse, *Critical Kit-Kats* (New York: Dodd, Mead and Co., 1896), 192–93.

4. Percy Fitzgerald, *The Book Fancier* (London: Sampson, Low, Marston and Co., n.d.), 124.

5. Oscar Wilde, *The Picture of Dorian Gray* (London: Penguin Books, 1973; originally published 1891), 142.

6. Fitzgerald, *The Book Fancier*, 124.

7. Ibid., 121–23.

8. Thomas Carlyle, as quoted in Holbrook Jackson, *The Anatomy of Bibliomania*, rev. ed. (New York: Scribner's Sons, 1932), 512.

9. Fitzgerald, *The Book Fancier*, 122.

10. E. Gordon Duff, *The Printers, Stationers and Bookbinders of Westminster and London from 1476 to 1535* (Cambridge: University Press, 1906), 106.

11. Thomas Frognall Dibdin, *Reminiscences of a Literary Life*, vol. 1 (London: John Major, 1836), 434–46.

12. Field, *Love Affairs of a Bibliomaniac*, vii.

13. A. Edward Newton, "On Forming a Library," in *Bouillabaisse for Bibliophiles*, ed. William Targ (Metuchen, NJ: Scarecrow Reprint Corp., 1955), 314–15.

Dr. Johnson: Book-Slob Extraordinaire

1. James Boswell, *The Life of Johnson* (New York: Penguin English Library, 1979; originally published 1791), 38.

2. Ibid., 41.

3. Ibid., 57.

4. Ibid., 65.

5. Ibid., 85.

6. Ibid., 213.

7. Ibid., 110.

8. Augustine Birrell, *Essays and Addresses*, vol. 1 (New York: Scribner's, 1923), 143–44.

9. Leslie Stephen, *Samuel Johnson* (New York: Harper & Brothers, 1879), 66.

10. Samuel Johnson, *Lives of the Poets*, cited in *Works*, vol. 11 (London: J. Haddon, 1820), 339–40.

Chapter THIRTEEN

1. Laman Blanchard, "The Art of Book-Keeping," in *Ballads of Books*, ed. Andrew Lang (London: Longmans, Green and Co., 1888), 51.
2. Holbrook Jackson, *The Anatomy of Bibliomania*, rev. ed. (New York: Scribner's Sons, 1932), 447.
3. Ibid.
4. Lawrence S. Thompson, "Notes on Biblio-kleptomania," in *Carrousel for Bibliophiles*, ed. William Targ (New York: Philip C. Duschnes, 1947), 122.
5. Falconer Madan, *Books in Manuscript* (London: Kegan Paul, Trench, Trubner & Co.; New York: Scribner's Sons, 1893), 90.
6. Richard de Bury, *The Love of Books: The Philobiblon*, trans. E. C. Thomas (London: Chatto & Windus, 1925; originally published 1473), 114–17.
7. John W. Clark, *The Care of Books* (Cambridge: University Press, 1901), 209.
8. W. J. Hardy, *Book-plates*, 2d ed. (London: Kegan Paul, Trench, Trubner & Co., 1897), 163.
9. Thompson, "Notes on Biblio-kleptomania," 139.

The Final Act

1. John Hill Burton, *The Book-Hunter*, ed. J. Herbert Slater (London: George Routledge & Sons; New York: E. P. Dutton & Co., n.d.), 9–11.

Chapter FOURTEEN

1. Holbrook Jackson, *The Anatomy of Bibliomania*, rev. ed. (New York: Scribner's Sons, 1932), 666.
2. Wendy Kaminer, "Chances Are You're Codependent Too," in *New York Times Book Review*, 11 Feb. 1990.
3. Eugene Field, *The Love Affairs of a Bibliomaniac* (New York: Scribner's Sons, 1896), 230.
4. F. Fertiault, "A Domestic Event," in *Ballads of Books*, ed. Andrew Lang (London: Longmans, Green and Co., 1888), 60.
5. George Gissing, *The House of Cobwebs* (New York: E. P. Dutton & Co., n.d.), 47–67.
6. William Blades, *The Enemies of Books* (London: Elliot Stock, 1902), 73.
7. Field, *The Love Affairs of a Bibliomaniac*, 145.

Bibliography

Adler, Mortimer J., and Charles Van Doren. *How to Read a Book*. 1940. Rev. ed. New York: Simon & Schuster, 1972.

Allan, P. B. M. *The Book-Hunter at Home*. New York: G. P. Putnam's Sons, 1920.

Archer, Richard, ed. *Rare Book Collections*. Association of College and Research Libraries Monograph Number 27. Chicago: American Library Association, 1965.

Armour, Richard. *The Happy Bookers*. New York: McGraw-Hill, 1976.

Bagbanes, Nicholas A. *A Gentle Madness: Bibliophiles, Bibliomanes, and the Eternal Passion for Books*. New York: Henry Holt & Co., 1995.

Beecher, Henry Ward. *Star Papers; or, Experiences of Art and Nature*. New York: J. C. Derby, 1885.

Birkerts, Sven. *The Gutenberg Elegies: The Fate of Reading in an Electronic Age*. New York: Fawcett Columbine, 1994.

———. *Readings*. Saint Paul, Minn.: Graywolf Press, 1999.

———, ed. *Tolstoy's Dictaphone: Technology and the Muse*. Saint Paul, Minn.: Graywolf Press, 1996.

Birrell, Augustine. *Essays and Addresses*. 3 vols. New York: Scribner's, 1923.

Blades, William. *The Enemies of Books*. London: Elliot Stock, 1902.

Boswell, James. *The Life of Johnson*. 1791. New York: Penguin English Library, 1979.

Brewer, Reginald. *The Delightful Diversion*. New York: Macmillan Co., 1935.

Burton, John Hill. *The Book-Hunter*. Edited by J. Herbert Slater. London: George Routledge & Sons; New York: E. P. Dutton & Co., n.d.

Carter, John. *ABC for Book Collectors*. London: Hart-Davis, 1952.

———. *Taste and Technique in Book Collecting*. 1948. London: Private Libraries Association, 1970.

Clark, John W. *The Care of Books*. Cambridge: University Press, 1901.

Cole, John Y., ed. *Books in Our Future: Perspectives and Proposals*. Washington: Library of Congress, 1987.

Colton, Charles Caleb. *Lacon, or, Many Things in a Few Words: Addressed to Those Who Think*. 1820. Rev. ed. New York: W. Gowans, 1855.

Currie, Barton. *Fishers of Books*. Boston: Little, Brown, & Co. 1931.

Davidson, Cathy N., ed. *Reading in America.* Baltimore: Johns Hopkins University Press, 1989.

de Bury, Richard. *The Love of Books: The Philobiblon.* 1473. Translated by E. C. Thomas. London: Chatto & Windus, 1925.

de Quincey, Thomas. *The Note Book of an English Opium-Eater.* Boston: James R. Osgood & Co., 1873.

de Ricci, Seymour. *English Collectors of Books & Manuscripts (1530–1930).* Cambridge: University Press, 1930.

Dibdin, Thomas Frognall. *Bibliomania.* London: McCreery, 1811.

———. *Reminiscences of a Literary Life.* 2 vols. London: John Major, 1836.

Duff, E. Gordon. *The Printers, Stationers and Bookbinders of* Westminster and London from 1476 to 1535. Cambridge: University Press, 1906.

Elton, Charles, and Mary Elton. *The Great Book-Collectors.* London: Kegan Paul, Trench, Trubner & Co., 1893.

Epstein, Jason. *Book Business: Publishing Past, Present, and Future.* New York: W. W. Norton & Co., 1985.

Epstein, Joseph. *Plausible Prejudices.* New York: W. W. Norton & Co., 1985.

———. *Once More around the Block.* New York: W. W. Norton & Co., 1987.

Everitt, Charles P. *The Adventures of a Treasure Hunter.* Boston: Little, Brown and Co., 1951.

Fadiman, Clifton. *The Lifetime Reading Plan.* 1960. 3d ed. New York: Harper & Row, Publishers, 1988.

Field, Eugene. *The Love Affairs of a Bibliomaniac.* New York: Scribner's Sons, 1896.

Fitzgerald, Percy. *The Book Fancier.* London: Sampson, Low, Marston and Co., n.d.

Fletcher, H. George, ed. *A Miscellany for Bibliophiles.* New York: Grastorf & Lang, 1979.

Gandert, Slade Richard. *Protecting Your Collection.* New York: The Haworth Press, 1982.

Gass, William H. *Habitations of the Word.* New York: Simon & Schuster, 1986.

Gilbar, Steven. *The Book Book.* New York: Bell Publishing Co., 1985.

Gissing, George. *The House of Cobwebs.* New York: E. P. Dutton & Co., n.d.

———. *The Private Papers of Henry Ryecroft.* London: Constable and Co., 1903.

Gosse, Edmund. *Critical Kit-Kats.* New York: Dodd, Mead and Co., 1896.

Hamilton, John Maxwell. *Casanova Was a Book Lover and Other Provocative Curiosities about the Writing, Selling, and Reading of Books.* Baton Rouge: Louisiana State University Press, 2000.

Bibliography

Hardy, W. J. *Book-plates*. 2d. ed. London: Kegan Paul, Trench, Trubner & Co., 1897.

Hinckley, Karen, and Barbara Hinckley. *American Best Sellers: A Reader's Guide to Popular Fiction*. Bloomington and Indianapolis: Indiana University Press, 1989.

Hornsby, Ken. *Is That the Library Speaking?* New York: St. Martin's Press, 1978.

Iacone, Salvatore J. *The Pleasures of Book Collecting*. New York: Harper & Row, Publishers, 1976.

Jackson, Holbrook. *The Anatomy of Bibliomania*. 1930. Rev. ed. New York: Scribner's Sons, 1932.

Jennison, Peter S., and Robert N. Sheridan, eds. *The Future of General Adult Books and Reading in America*. Chicago: American Library Association, 1970.

Johns, Adrian. *The Nature of the Book: Print and Knowledge in the Making*. Chicago: University of Chicago Press, 1998.

Koch, Theodore W., ed. *Tales for Bibliophiles*. 1929. Reprint. Freeport, NY: Books for Libraries Press, 1972.

Lamb, Charles. *The Essays of Elia*. New York: A. C. Armstrong & Son, 1888.

Lang, Andrew. *The Library*. London: Macmillan & Co., 1881.

———, ed. *Ballads of Books*. London and New York: Longmans, Green, and Co., 1888.

Lewis, Wilmarth. *Collector's Progress*. New York: Alfred A. Knopf, 1951.

Locker-Lampson, Frederick. *My Confidences: An Autobiographical Sketch Addressed to My Descendants*. 2d ed. London: Smith, Elder, & Co., 1896.

Madan, Falconer. *Books in Manuscript*. London: Kegan Paul, Trench, Trubner & Co; New York: Scribner's Sons, 1893.

Manguel, Alberto. *A History of Reading*. New York: Viking Penguin, 1996.

Marvin, Frederic Rowland. *The Excursions of a Book-Lover*. Boston: Sherman, French & Co., 1910.

Matthews, Jack. *Booking in the Heartland*. Baltimore: Johns Hopkins University Press, 1986.

Merryweather, F. Somner. *Bibliomania in the Middle Ages*. New York: Meyer Brothers & Co., 1900.

Meyer, Lewis. *The Customer Is Always*. Garden City, NY: Doubleday & Co., 1965.

Newton, A. Edward. *The Amenities of Book-Collecting and Kindred Affections*. Boston: Atlantic Monthly Press, 1918.

———. *A Magnificent Farce*. 1921. Freeport, NY: Books for Libraries Press, 1970.

Parsons, Nicholas. *The Book of Literary Lists*. New York: Facts on File Publications, 1987.

Peters, Jean, ed. *Book Collecting: A Modern Guide*. New York: R. R. Bowker Co., 1977.

Petroski, Henry. *The Book on the Book Shelf*. New York: Alfred A. Knopf, 1999.

Powell, Lawrence Clark. *A Passion for Books*. Cleveland: World Publishing Co., 1958.

——. *Books in my Baggage*. Cleveland: World Publishing Co., 1960.

Quindlen, Anna. *How Reading Changed My Life*. New York: Library of Contemporary Thought, Ballantine Publishing Group, 1998.

Rosebery, Archibald Philip Primrose. *Miscellanies Literary & Historical*. 2 vols. London: Hodder and Stoughton, 1921.

Rosenbach, A.S.W. *Books and Bidders*. Boston: Little, Brown, and Co., 1927.

——. *A Book Hunter's Holiday*. Boston and New York: Houghton Mifflin, 1936.

Rostenberg, Leona, and Madeleine B. Stern. *Between Boards: New Thoughts on Old Books*. Montclair, NJ: Allanheld & Schram, 1978.

Schiffrin, Andre. *The Business of Books*. New York: Verso, 2000.

Schwarz, Lynne Sharon. *Ruined by Reading: A Life in Books*. Boston: Beacon Press, 1996.

Smith, Logan Pearsall. *All Trivia*. New York: Harcourt, Brace and Co., 1945.

Smith, Roger H., ed. *The American Reading Public: What It Reads, Why It Reads*. New York: R. R. Bowker Co., 1962.

Spence, Joseph. *Observations, Anecdotes, and Characters of Books and Men*. 1771. Edited by James M. Osborn. 2 vols. Oxford: Clarendon Press, 1966.

Spencer, Walter T. *Forty Years in My Bookshop*. Boston and New York: Houghton Mifflin, 1923.

Squire, John Collings. *Essays at Large*. 1922. Port Washington, NY: Kennikat Press, 1968.

Starrett, Vincent. *Penny Wise and Book Foolish*. New York: Covici Friede, 1929.

Targ, William, ed. *Carrousel for Bibliophiles*. New York: Philip C. Duschnes, 1947.

——, ed. *Bouillabaisse for Bibliophiles*. Metuchen, NJ: Scarecrow Reprint Corp., 1955.

Trevelyan, G. O. *The Life and Letters of Lord Macaulay*. 2 vols. New York: Harper & Brothers, 1904.

Tuleja, Tad. *The Catalog of Lost Books*. New York: Fawcett Columbine, 1989.

West, Herbert Faulkner. *Modern Book Collecting for the Impecunious Amateur*. Boston: Little, Brown, and Co., 1936.

Wilson, Robert A. *Modern Book Collecting*. New York: Alfred A. Knopf, 1980.

About the Author

TOM RAABE, A DEDICATED BIBLIOHOLIC, has taught Yankee sports to Australian high schoolers and worked for newspapers in Portland, Maine, and San Diego. In his book-free days, he was still able to travel and visited Indonesia, Singapore, India, Nepal, Afghanistan, Iran, Turkey, and Europe. For the last decade or so, he has worked as a freelance editor and writer in Denver, Colorado.